Global Environmental Change:
Biodiversity

Biodiversity is the first installment in the *Global Environmental Change Series,* which the National Science Teachers Association is developing in conjunction with the U.S. Environmental Protection Agency. Future books will also use case studies to focus on such global issues as deforestation, solid waste management, and population growth.

The *Global Environmental Change Series* is science based, and links the ecology and biology of global changes with insights from other disciplines. The series encourages students to weigh a wide range of relevant information from pertinent disciplines, and to develop their own opinions in order to make their own decisions.

Global Environmental Change:
Biodiversity

A vast diversity of biological species inhabit Earth. Estimates of Earth's total species diversity range from 10–100 million. Yet the number of species scientists have actually classified is only 1,413,000. More than 751,000 are insects, and about 248,000 are higher plants. The pie chart below roughly depicts the numbers of species that have been scientifically described.

The range of estimates of Earth's total biodiversity is so broad because we know so little about certain kingdoms of organisms, particularly the Monera and Protista. Only about 31,000 protozoa species, 5,000 bacteria species, and 1,000 species of viruses have been classified. Certain ecosystems, such as rain forest canopies and ocean floors, remain relatively unexplored.

But even unexplored ecosystems are being altered by human activity in unprecedented ways.

During the Industrial Revolution, people began realizing that the relationship between humans and ecosystems was changing. Where ecosystems once defined and changed people, people were now defining and changing ecosystems.

Many human-induced global environmental changes may not be fully apparent for generations. Researchers point to species eradication as one of the most profound effects of human action on natural systems. Ecosystems are complex, interactive webs of diverse relationships among biologically distinct species. These relationships are eroding faster over the past two centuries than at any time since the dinosaurs died out about 65 million years ago.

What Is Biodiversity?

Biodiversity refers to the variety of biological species, the genetic differences among them, and the habitats and ecosystems they comprise. A species is any population whose members interbreed freely under natural conditions. The concept of biodiversity goes well beyond a mere catalog of living organisms, embracing the breadth and interrelatedness of all life on Earth.

Insects
751,000

Other
Animals
281,000

Higher
Plants
248,400

Fungi
69,000

Viruses
1,000

Living Species Currently
Known to Science

Protozoa
30,800

Monera
4,800

Algae
26,900

The Case Study:
Biodiversity in Costa Rica

One threat to Earth's biodiversity is the idea that "progress" means an ever-expanding command over natural resources. Economic growth, for example, has traditionally been linked to control over natural resources through agriculture, mining, and forestry. Until quite recently, the ecological health and biological integrity of a natural resource base have been left out of the economic growth equation.

Current thinking about progress recognizes that growth shouldn't occur at the expense of a nation's natural resources, but should instead rely on resource conservation and renewability. This definition of progress is especially relevant among those "developing" nations that want to balance resource conservation with economic growth.

Costa Rica provides an excellent case study of one nation's commitment to balancing resource conservation and economic growth. In 1985, Costa Rica reached a crisis which could have resulted in the loss of its remaining tropical forests to agricultural and economic development. But the government mounted an effort to rechannel national economic energies. Recognizing the economic value of biological diversity, Costa Rica is preserving what remains.

Roughly the size of West Virginia, Costa Rica is a mountainous Central American nation with a dramatically varied geography that includes 12 ecologically distinct ecosystems. Costa Rica is home to 850 bird species—more than the United States and Canada combined—and over 12,000 plant species. In all, more than 50,000 biological species inhabit Costa Rica's 51,000 square kilometers.

Costa Rica (below) is a Central American nation that is developing a model for balancing natural resource conservation with economic growth.

Study Area: Costa Rica

To protect and conserve its natural resources, Costa Rica established a national park system and initiated a nationwide biodiversity survey. It has redefined relationships with multinational corporations by trading access to natural resources for advanced technology, and by setting legal precedents for property rights and patents resulting from product development. Through these and other efforts, Costa Rica has turned itself into a laboratory for the global scientific community. The activities in this book use Costa Rica as a case study for engaging your students in the scientific investigation of biological diversity.

3

Defining Biodiversity

Objective
To define biodiversity as the number of biological species present in an ecosystem.

Background

We don't have to go to a tropical forest to learn about biodiversity. We can study it in any ecosystem on Earth: the seashore, a forest floor, swamp mud, even a pinecone. Our challenge is to observe and identify all the organisms that live together in an ecosystem. In this activity, students will first measure and then analyze the species diversity of a nearby ecosystem—the old cones dropped by conifers in a wooded area. Students will learn that many different species of organisms live within the ecosystem of a fallen cone.

Biodiversity is one of those natural phenomena that should be experienced directly to be understood and appreciated. Students can, of course, read about the richness and diversity of communities within various ecosystems. They can watch videos about tropical forests and be moved emotionally by reports of biodiversity loss and its consequences. But can they link their emotional and philosophical reactions to the causes and effects, to the science that underlies the concept of biological diversity? And can they use science as one among many tools when they debate issues pertaining to natural resource conservation and economic growth?

This may seem like a lot to ask of high-school-age students. But the apparent conflict between conservation and growth is exactly the kind of serious question that will occupy some of your students as they make their way in the world. Until students, even high school students, have authentic, science-based, multisensory, and engaging experiences with biological diversity, their understanding will remain anecdotal at best.

This activity enables students—and teachers—to get their hands dirty with biodiversity. By manipulating the cone ecosystem, its inhabitant species, and the Berlese separator, students learn that biodiversity means the number of species present in an ecosystem. Upon understanding this definition of what biodiversity physically is, they will be prepared to progress through this book's activities.

Time Management
This activity may be organized according to the following schedule:

Day 1
Collect cones, construct and set up separator, run for 3–7 days.

Day 2
Examine, sort, and count specimens. Compile data, discuss.

Procedure

1. Have students gather a grocery bag full of weathered cones from the ground beneath one or several conifer trees, or gather them yourself in advance. Conifers will likely be found in woods, a cemetery, or a park.

2. Using the assembled materials, have students set up a Berlese separator as depicted in Figure 1, or construct it yourself in advance.

Figure 1

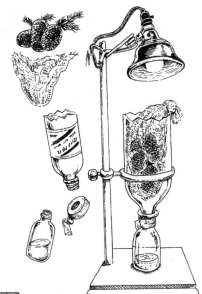

3. In the laboratory, have students place as many cones as will fit on the screen, or in the cheesecloth bag, in the separator's funnel. Have them switch on the lamp and allow the separator to run uninterrupted for 3–7 days, or until specimens stop falling into the collecting jar (Figure 2).

Materials
- Berlese separator
  - Cheese cloth
  - 2 l plastic soda bottle
  - Small lamp
  - Ring stand
  - Clamps
  - Small jar
  - 70% ethanol
  - Duct tape
  - Petri dish
- Dissecting microscope
- Medicine dropper
- Dissecting needle
- Finepointed paint brush
- Small vials, corks
- Conifer cones
- Guide to Cone Critters (page 11)
- Student Worksheets

Figure 2
The organisms living in the fallen cones leave the cone's shelter as the lamp's heat dries out their surroundings. When they emerge from the cones the animals move down and away from the heat and light, falling through the screen into the jar where they are preserved in the alcohol.

What is a species?

The concept of biodiversity is not problem free. One source of controversy stems from ambiguity about what a species is. A generally accepted definition is that a species is a population whose members interbreed freely under natural conditions. But there are exceptions to and difficulties with nearly every part of this definition, all interesting and all debatable. What, for example, is a "natural condition"? What constitutes "freely" interbreeding when human activity has so effectively altered the global environment?

Table 1
Fifty Douglas fir cones were collected from Sehome Hill near Bellingham, Washington, in January, 1995, to compile this data set. Drawings of the species appear on page 11, but it is recommended that they not be shown to students until they have produced their own drawings, as they might detract from observing, describing, and sketching on their own.

4. Students may now transfer the specimens from the alcohol into a petri dish. Several alcohol rinsings may be needed to completely clear the jar. A fine-pointed paint brush wetted in alcohol will collect any specimens remaining on the jar's sides.

5. Have students examine the contents of the petri dish with a dissecting microscope. Most of the animals they find are probably such arthropods as mites, spiders, millipedes, centipedes, and pseudoscorpions. Have students use a dissecting needle to sort the specimens according to species. Best guesses will suffice.

6. Have students count the number of different species they find in their cones. The number of different species they identify is a measure of the cone ecosystem's biodiversity.

7. Now have students count the number of individuals within each species. The number of individuals within a species is a measure of the species' population size, or its abundance.

8. Have students create worksheets using the model provided as Table 1 (left). Have them record their data about biodiversity and population abundances on their worksheets.

9. Have students compare and contrast their data with data compiled by their classmates. The questions beginning on the next page outline general parameters for a class discussion.

Table 1
Diversity and Populations in Douglas Fir Cones

Organism	Number of Species	Population Size
pseudoscorpion	1	13
pselaphognath	1	23
centipede	1	3
millipede	1	1
mites	7+	182 total
sp. A		96
sp. B		25
sp. C		1
sp. D		15
sp. E		20
sp. F		5
sp. G		10
sp. misc.		10
collembola	5+	245 total
sp. A		16
sp. B		54
sp. C		21
sp. D		125
sp. E		6
sp. misc.		23
beetles	3	8 total
sp. weevil		1
sp. ladybug		4
sp. larvae		3
spiders	3	3 total
sp. A		1
sp. B		1
sp. C		1
earthworm	1	1
unidentified	X	5

What is a food web?

Ecologists arrange all plants and animals among four basic feeding groups, or trophic levels—primary producers, herbivores, carnivores, and decomposers—in their modeling of how energy flows through ecosystems. This is a descriptive model; actual trophic relationships in nature aren't straight-line chains.

Another model is the food web, many chains interlinked within and among ecosystems. But translating trophic theories about energy flow into food web theories is difficult because some organisms feed on more than one level. Single species seldom live exclusively by consuming another single species. Energy resources tend to be shared among many organisms. How can we measure the energy a species contributes to each of the trophic levels it occupies? How do species with different consumption habits at different life stages figure into determining how many levels exist?

Ecologists working with such questions now think of species that have the same diets and predators in a food web as belonging to one trophic level. They arrange all the species in a food web accordingly, assigning them to basal, intermediate, and top trophic levels. Basal species feed on only one level and top species have no predators. Intermediate species feed on more than one level.

Questions for Discussion

1. Ask students why they think the animal communities in the cones they examined are so diverse? Couldn't just several animals do a better job of living in that ecosystem than several dozen?

2. Students probably found the greatest diversity among springtails and mites. One of ecology's primary themes is that each species in an ecosystem occupies a role, or niche, distinct from all other species. How can so many mite species live so closely in the cones under one tree?

3. Have students consider what the food web of the cone's animal community might look like. How does the cone ecosystem food web differ from food webs of ecosystems with low diversity, or few animal species? With high diversity, or many animal species? Have students make sketches of such food webs.

4. Ask students what the population sizes of the cone's organisms tells them about the role of those organisms in the cone ecosystem food web? Suppose they consistently found over 100 individuals of one species and only several individuals of another species. How might the feeding role of the two species differ? What would be their likely positions in the food web?

5. Have students make a sketch of how energy flows through the community of cone organisms. They may use Figure 3, which depicts how energy flows through a wetland ecosystem, as a model.

Figure 3
Energy flow in a simplified wetland ecosystem. Energy flows from the sun through plants, herbivores, and carnivores. Decomposers—chiefly bacteria, protozoa, and fungi—derive energy from all three trophic levels.

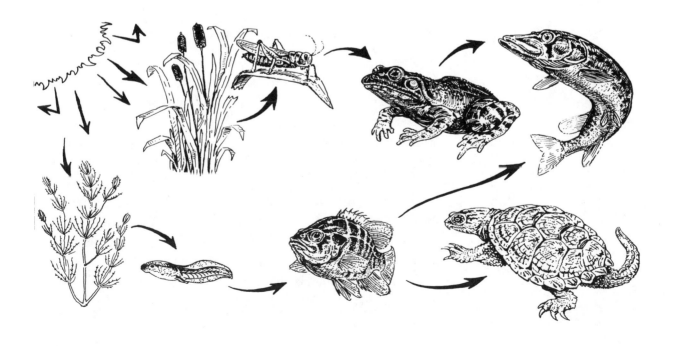

How does energy flow through an ecosystem?

In physics, the First Law of Thermodynamics states that energy is neither created nor destroyed, but changes form when transferred from one component to another. One of ecology's central themes is that the First Law holds true for ecosystems. As energy flows from plants and herbivores to carnivores and decomposers, its form changes, but it is never created nor destroyed.

The Second Law of Thermodynamics states that during an energy transfer some energy assumes a form that cannot pass further. For example, heat energy escapes from a system. The Second Law applies to closed systems that don't exchange energy with their surroundings. Ecosystems do not conform to the Second Law because they are wide open, and constantly exchange energy with other systems.

6. Some ecosystems, like tropical forests, have extremely high biodiversity while others, like taiga forests, have quite low biodiversity. Ask students what factors are most important in affecting biodiversity in natural environments? How have humans influenced biodiversity in environments of which we are a part?

7. Have students suppose the population of one of the species of mites drops below the level where it can successfully reproduce. The species is declared to be endangered, and its extinction is likely unless special conservation measures are enforced.

Who cares? At least 500,000 species of mites exist on Earth. Perhaps less than a dozen people in the world are even aware of this particular mite's existence. Why should we care that a tiny, inconspicuous, and relatively unknown animal faces extinction as a direct result of human activity? Who among us would disagree, and why?

Answers to Discussion Questions

1. Ecosystems with low diversity are less stable—and therefore more vulnerable to disruption—than ecosystems with high diversity. Suppose the primary producer is a potato, the herbivore a potato beetle, and the beetle-eating predator is a species of barn swallow. A single disruption, such as a fungus infection in the potato's leaves, might cause a serious disruption in this small food web. On the other hand, suppose a food web contained 83 species of plants, 49 species of herbivores—including insects, millipedes, rabbits, field mice, slugs, fungus, and bacteria—and 20 species of carnivores—including foxes, dragon flies, hawks, owls, and snakes. A disease affecting blue jays would have a disruptive impact on this food web, but the potential threat to the entire ecosystem would be minimized. The greater the diversity in an ecosystem, the smaller the holes in its safety net.

2. The primary source of nutritional energy on the forest floor is decomposing plant material, fungus, bacteria, and juices in living roots and other animals. Spring tails and mites feed at these "troughs." Their food is so varied and abundant that the mites and spring tails have evolved special structures and physiologies that have enabled them to become separate kinds of organisms. Although the species coexist inside a cone, they live quite separate lives, and are kept distinct by the reproductive isolation that ensures the genetic integrity of their individual species.

3. The three sketches of food webs (Figure 4) provide examples of representative food webs in ecosystems with low, moderate, and high diversity. The cones in this activity are an example of an ecosystem with moderate diversity.

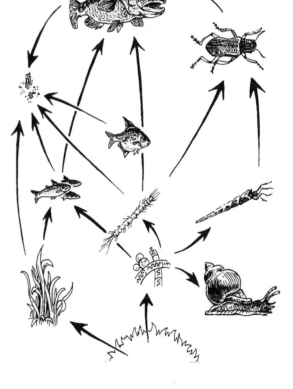

Low Diversity

Moderate Diversity

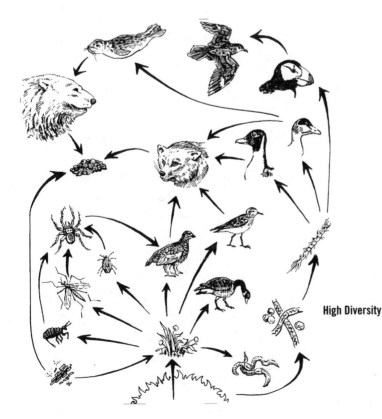

High Diversity

Figure 4
Representative food webs in ecosystems with low, moderate, and high diversity.

4. Students might hypothesize that the numbers or masses of individuals of a species occur in proportion to the amount of food consumed. Thus, in the example used, the 100 specimens of a single species may suggest a herd-like grazing niche. Perhaps these arthropods feed on a field of plant debris. The several species may represent the few predatory centipedes or pseudoscorpions.

5. As will hold true of student energy flow sketches, the representative food webs in Figure 4 are based on hypothetical ecosystems.

6. In their discussion of factors that ensure healthy biodiversity, students should identify such essential components of the environment as energy, pure water, pure air, and an absence of damaging radiation.

7. Invoke the snail darter debate, which may be summarized by stating that each human-caused species extinction diminishes all other species. Students may also analyze the "Humans First" philosophy, which contends that human happiness, health, comfort, prosperity, and recreation have more intrinsic value than an individual or collection of other species. Explore potential relationships among species diversity and human well-being.

Suggestions for Further Study

• Similar results can be achieved by filling the separator with measured quantities of leaf litter from a woodland floor. The separator technique is more managable than building a platform over a forest canopy, and taxonomists inventorying Costa Rican biodiversity use variations of the Berlese separator used in this activity. Students should be encouraged to consider that they are engaged in an authentic, sophisticated scientific investigation similar to those being conducted in Costa Rica.

• Have students explore how biodiversity and population size changes with the seasons of the year in the cones at one location in a forest. Have students form and test a hypothesis about the diversity of cone life under trees at higher altitudes.

• Another area to explore pertains to whether the cone organisms colonized the cones before or after the cones fell from their trees. Have students pluck the same number of cones from the same trees under which they collect fallen cones. Conduct identical investigations on both sets of cones and compare the two data sets. This comparative technique provides a means of highlighting the importance of proper scientific methodology.

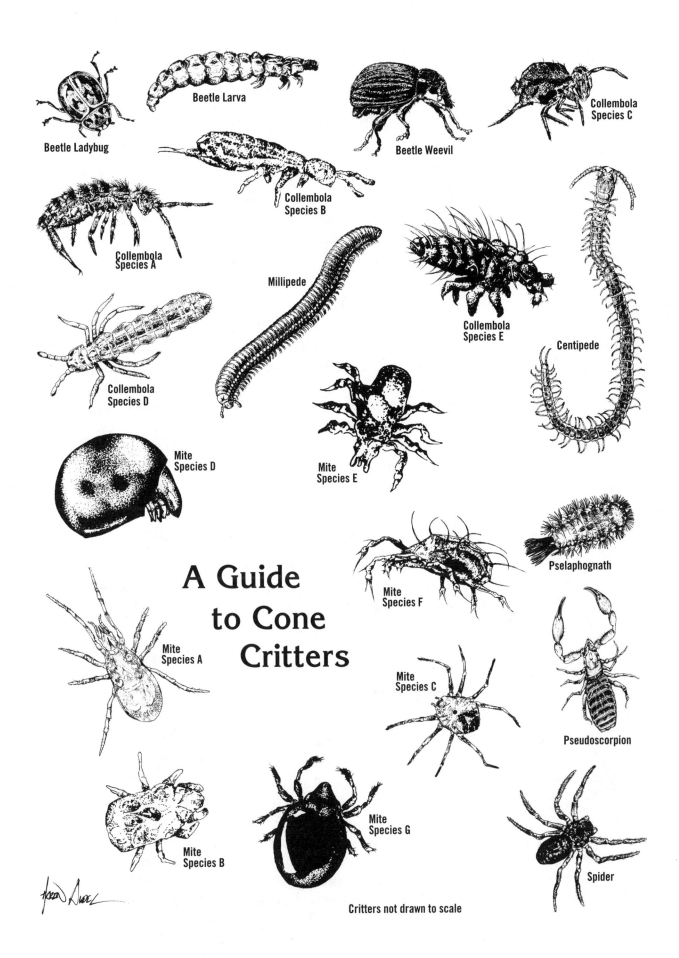

Beetle Ladybug

Beetle Larva

Beetle Weevil

Collembola Species C

Collembola Species B

Collembola Species A

Collembola Species D

Millipede

Collembola Species E

Centipede

Mite Species D

Mite Species E

Pselaphognath

Mite Species F

A Guide to Cone Critters

Mite Species A

Mite Species C

Pseudoscorpion

Mite Species B

Mite Species G

Spider

Critters not drawn to scale

Quantifying Biodiversity

Objective
To teach students scientific methodology for quantifying biodiversity and estimating rates of species extinction due to habitat loss.

Background

This activity is divided into three Parts. In Part A, students learn how to conduct a systematic biodiversity inventory by collecting, organizing, and analyzing species data from a lawn habitat. In Part B, students apply math skills—the species-area equation—to first determine the relationship between how many species they find and the size of the ecosystem they inventory. They then use a variation of the species-area equation to estimate species extinction rates within that discrete ecosystem. In Part C, students apply the data they developed in Parts A and B toward designing a sanctuary to preserve their habitat's biodiversity.

Time Management
In Part A, you may want to conduct the preliminary site survey and mark off the area for study prior to the activity, which may be completed in a class period. Student involvement in all portions of the activity will, of course, increase their understanding of methodology. Parts B and C together should take about two class periods.

Part A: Systematic Inventory and Data Collection

In Part A, students first collect and organize data about plant species diversity by making a systematic inventory of a habitat they're familiar with—a lawn. They then organize and analyze the data they collected, and apply mathematical skills to estimate the lawn's biodiversity.

Procedure

Materials
Twine
Stakes
Blank paper, pencils
Meter sticks
Field guide to local wildflowers
  and plants

1. Select an established lawn with at least a three-year-old grass cover that receives little attention other than mowing. Don't choose a newly planted or sodded lawn, as it will likely contain only a single species.

2. To verify that your site has sufficient biodiversity, have students conduct a preliminary survey by slowly walking in a line for about 25–50 paces. Have them count and note the different plants they encounter. Positive identification isn't necessary at this point. If the preliminary survey reveals at least 12 different species, have students establish a 64m^2 site. If the survey yields fewer than 10 species, select another site.

3. Once your survey site is selected, divide the class among the following four job descriptions: one group of surveyors, two groups of collectors, and one group of identifiers. Assign the surveyors the task of using stakes and twine to lay out the site in one-meter segments (Figure 1). Have the collectors bring all samples to a central "museum," where the identifiers will create a catalog of the site's species diversity. Depending on the size of the class, the surveyors may also maintain the "museum," or they may join in collecting samples.

Students will need to get down on their hands and knees to make their inventories. They will also need to be careful not to trample the site too severely, as this might make them miss some significant species. Encourage students to develop a system for working as a team. One way to do this might be to have them pretend they are a team of scientists making a taxonomic inventory of an unknown, unusual, or endangered site.

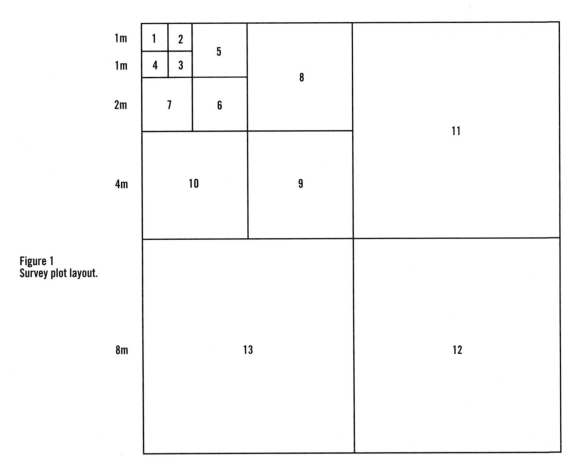

Figure 1
Survey plot layout.

4. Have the collectors retrieve a sample of each plant species, record the quadrat where each sample came from, and bring all the samples to the "museum." The museum group may then compile the data using a Data Summary Sheet like the one in Figure 2 on the next page.

5. When the surveying and identifying teams have completed their tasks, have the museum team organize the data into a finalized Data Summary Sheet.

Figure 2
Sample Data Summary Sheet. These data came from a site in Olathe, Kansas, that was about three years old at the time of the inventory. X denotes the first time a species was recorded in a nested plot, and + denotes each time thereafter.

QUADRAT NUMBER

SPECIES	1	2	3	4	5	6	7	8	9	10	11	12	13
Nut grass	X	+	+	+	+	+	+	+	+	+	+	+	+
Cat whiskers		X		+	+				+	+		+	+
Purple top grass	X	+		+						+			+
Baby hairless clover	X	+	+		+	+	+		+	+		+	+
Giant fuzzy clover	X	+	+		+	+	+	+	+		+	+	+
Foxtail					X		+	+		+		+	+
Wheat		X			+			+					
Pokey thin wheat								X				+	+
Tube grass					X			+					
Saplings								X			+	+	+
Cactus						X	+	+	+	+	+	+	+
Daisy										X			
Bedhead										X	+	+	+
Triangle clover											X	+	+
Lab ear											X	+	+
Bunny ear											X		
Red stem pot													X
Red stem bell											X		
Puffball fungus											X		
Parsley				X									
Caesar salad leaf						X			+	+		+	+
Bunched nut grass									X	+	+		
Velvet lizard tongue							X					+	
Furry fingers												X	
Pod grass				X			+		+	+		+	+
Small grapefruit spoon									X				
Large grapefruit spoon				X			+			+		+	+
Broom grass									X				
Furry lace													X
Moss												X	+
Tree							X						
Total Per Block	4	6	3	6	7	5	9	8	10	12	11	17	18
Cumulative Total	4	6	6	9	11	13	15	17	20	22	27	29	31
Area of Block	1	1	1	1	4	4	4	16	16	16	64	64	64
Cumulative Area	1	2	3	4	8	12	16	32	48	64	128	192	256

6. Have students analyze their data to look for patterns. For this data set, there are a number of fruitful areas to explore. For example: have students compare the plants in the study site to plants in nearby habitats that are ecologically distinct from the lawn. Are nearby areas wetter or drier, sunnier or shadier, flatter or more sloped? How might these factors account for differences in observed species?

7. The nested sampling plots provide a means to visualize the relationship between the number of plant species to the size of the habitat area. The easiest way to do this is to make a graph comparing the total number of plant species to the total area of the sampling plots. (This graphing can also be done with a computer spreadsheet program.) Figure 3 is a sample graph using data from Figure 2.

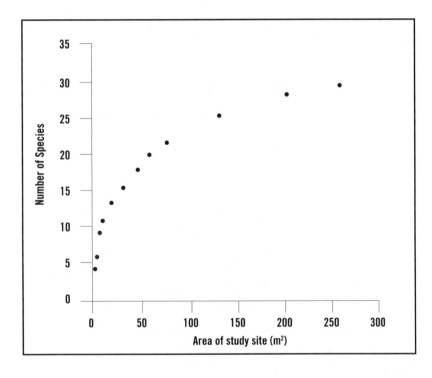

Figure 3
Sample graph using data from Figure 2. The graph depicts a classic species-area curve.

What is the species-area equation?

Students may wonder how scientists developed the species-area equation. Often, mathematical expressions are the result of theoretical work, but in this case the species-area equation is the result of a lot of experimental field and lab work. For many organisms and communities, this equation simply fits the data.
    Figure 3 is a geometric example of the relationship between geographic area surveyed and number of species found. The general shape of the curve is typical, although its precise shape would vary with the biology and natural history of the area being studied. In the example shown, a doubling of the area surveyed adds only about 25 percent to the number of species. The species-area relationship is widely used among conservation biologists in predicting the number of extinctions that will result from reduction of habitat area.

Part B: The Species-Area Equation

In Part A, students made a graph to depict the species-area relationship in the lawn habitat. This relationship may also be expressed algebraically using the species-area equation: $S = cA^z$. This equation's premise is simple: the number of species increases in direct proportion to the size of the area. By sampling the total number of species in a small area, the total number of species in a larger area may be extrapolated.

Scientists use the species-area equation to make predictions about the ecological impacts of human activity, such as the rate of species extinction due to habitat loss. In Part B, students will use the species-area equation to test the accuracy of their graphs of the species-area relationship in the lawn habitat—the "best-fit" curve they made in Part A. They will then use it to estimate rates of species extinction when the size of the lawn habitat is reduced.

Procedure

1. Write out the species-area equation on the chalkboard, and tell students they will be using it to interpret the data they collected from the lawn habitat inventory. The species-area equation is as follows:

$$S = cA^z$$
S = the total number of species
A = the total area surveyed
c and z are constants that pertain to the ecological makeup of the community of organisms under study

2. Ask students if they know how scientists make estimates about species loss at global levels. How can scientists estimate the rate at which Earth's biological species are disappearing if they haven't inventoried all of them yet? Tell students that scientists use the species-area equation to make such estimates, and that they're going to use it to estimate species extinction rates due to habitat loss in the lawn habitat they just inventoried. By reducing the size of the lawn habitat, they will estimate how that reduction has impacted the habitat's total number of species.

3. Have students check their graphically derived answer for their minimum sample survey by using the species-area equation. To do this, they must first solve for c. Have students use the following values to practice using the species-area equation and to see how it works.

let z = 0.30 (see sidebar, below)
let S = 25 (number of species)
let A = 256 (16m^2 x 16m^2 = 256m^2, the values from Figure 1)

$$25 = c256^{0.30}$$
$$25/256^{0.30} = c256^{0.30}/256^{0.30}$$
$$25/256^{0.30} = c$$
$$4.7 = c$$

4. Now have students reduce the size of the lawn habitat by 25 percent, as might occur through habitat loss, to find out how many species remain.

$$(75\%)(256m^2) = 192m^2$$
$$A \text{ (area)} = 192m^2$$
$$S = cA^z$$
$$S = (4.7)(192^{0.30})$$
$$S = 22.7$$

This is essentially the same answer as derived from the graph in Figure 3. If student answers don't match, have them recheck their calculations. If their answers still don't match, have them speculate on which might be more accurate: the slope of their graph or the species-area equation. (Most likely, they didn't draw a smooth enough curve between their graph's data points.)

What are the c and z values?

Different ecosystems have different biotic and abiotic components, as well as different relationships among those components. A tropical forest, for example, is made up of different biotic and abiotic components than a deciduous forest. It is necessary to factor those differences into the species-area equation when using it to differentiate between ecological developments among ecosystems, such as species extinction rates due to habitat loss. The c and z values provide variables for accomplishing this algebraically.

The species-area relationship was first formalized in the 1920s by Olaf Arrhenius, and a veritable library of ecological literature has since been written debating the meaning of the mathematical constants by which the species-area relationship can be algebraically described. Empirical studies among many diverse groups

of organisms during the 1960s and 1970s revealed that most values for z fall within a range of 0.20 and 0.35.

The relative consistency for the z value suggests two possibilities: (a) that observed values for z might be the result of a simple statistical consequence of the lognormal distribution of species abundances; and (b) habitat heterogeneity increases with the size and consequent topographic heterogeniety of a study area.

For the purposes of this activity, however, it isn't necessary for students to be fully acquainted with all the ramifications of the ongoing ecological debate about the c and z constants and their algebraic function in the species-area dynamic. If you wish, students can derive the z value for the lawn habitat using their own data, or they may simply use the value, .30, as described in the procedure.

Part C: Applying Data to Preserving Biodiversity

Procedure

Materials
pencil
paper

Have the class assume that the study site is an endangered ecosystem. Ask them to design a sanctuary for lawn plants that would conserve as many plant species as possible. Tell students that all the plants in the lawn habitat have at least some "value," that they are all worth saving. Student design proposals should include the following components:

How do scientists estimate global biodiversity loss?

Ecologists are continually trying to answer the question of whether current rates of global biodiversity loss are normal or abnormal. Scientists use the exponential z value to estimate global species extinction rates due to cumulative habitat reduction and loss. But first, they must estimate rates of global habitat loss. At the current rate of tropical deforestation, for example, less than 50 percent of Earth's current tropical forest will exist by 2025. That's a loss of about 50 percent of the current total area of global tropical forest, which is $8 \times 10^6 km^2$. Applying the species-area equation to current global tropical forest area results in the equation:

$$5 \text{ million} = cA^{0.30}$$

Applying the species-area equation to current deforested tropical forest area results in the equation:

$$S = c[A/2]^{0.30}$$

Dividing equation 1 by equation 2 results in the following equation, where S equals the number of remaining species:

$$5 \text{ million}/S = 2^{0.30}$$

Solving for S means 4 million species remaining in the year 2025, the same as saying that 20 percent of global tropical forest species will become extinct over the next 30 years.

This is a very conservative estimate, as the equation takes into account only area effects. Other phenomena also lead to extinction of species. The species-area equation depicts an estimated species extinction rate among tropical forests of approximately 33,000 species per year, which means about 90 species per day or four species an hour. Some argue that this extinction rate is natural and that organisms are simply not adapting fast enough to human changes. Evidence found in the fossil record is used by some to support this contention (see What are mass extinctions?, page 39). Others, however, argue that this is an alarming extinction rate. Ecologist E.O. Wilson has pointed to this rate of species extinction as humankind's single biggest potential catastrophe.

• Descriptions of the types of plants to be found in their sanctuary. Descriptions should consider whether a plant is, for example, primarily a lawn species (grasses), a cosmopolitan plant (dandelions), or an accidental (trees).

• The number of species that would survive in various, different-sized sanctuaries. Student analyses should contain at least three cases.

• Predictions about the species that would not be preserved and why. Best guesses will suffice.

• A recommendation as to the first and second choice for the "ideal" sanctuary size. Students should use their graphs from Part A to choose a target percentage of species to arrive at their recommendations.

• Notes on potential and real threats—other than habitat reduction—that might reduce their sanctuary's biodiversity.

• Ecological comparisons with adjacent "ecosystems."

Questions for Discussion

Part A: Systematic Inventory and Data Collection

1. Have students analyze their data. How many total species are there? How many in each quadrat? How many per square meter? Are the number of species evenly spread throughout the study site, or are they clustered within a certain quadrat? Looking at the site's environmental condition, are there reasons why plants are spread out or clustered?

2. Students should look at the graphs they constructed showing how the number of species changes as the area increases. Is the relationship directly proportional?

3. Looking at the graph, have students determine how large a plot would be needed in order to be certain it included 75 percent of the total species present in the community.

4. Have students look at the area adjacent to the study site. Are conditions the same or similar? If the size of the study site were doubled, would the number of species increase or not? Why or why not?

5. If you have conducted this activity with two or more classes, have them compare their respective maps. Are their findings more or less compatible? What would account for any differences?

Part B: Using the Species-Area Equation

1. What is the rate of species extinction if the size of the lawn habitat is reduced by 50 percent?

2. What are some factors besides habitat reduction that could affect species extinction rates, especially in larger ecosystems?

Part C: Applying Data to Preserving Biodiversity

1. Would the entire lawn habitat need to be protected in order to preserve all its species from extinction?

2. If the entire habitat were preserved, should a wide sidewalk be allowed to be constructed through it? How might it affect the sanctuary's biodiversity? Why?

3. What other factors, besides habitat size, affect a site's biodiversity? Have students draw on what they've learned during this activity, and link it to information they've acquired from other sources.

Answers to Discussion Questions

Part A: Systematic Inventory and Data Collection

1. Answers will depend on the nature of the site, but there should be at least 12 species, with variations among each quadrat and per square meter. Conditions that could lead to clustering might include: (a) part of the study site is shaded; (b) part is adjacent to a parking lot or sidewalk; (c) part is at a lower elevation; and (d) part is rockier or sandier. Where conditions are consistent throughout the plot, it's likely the number of species among each quadrat will also be fairly consistent.

2. The relationship is proportional, but not 1:1. The curve is a classic species-area configuration; it makes sense that, as a sampling area increases in a community, such as an urban lawn, most will eventually be counted. However, if most of the species present are counted by the time 50 percent of the site is inventoried, the rate of new discoveries will slow as an inventory of 100 percent of the site is neared.

3. On their graphs, have students locate the number of species equivalent to 75 percent of the total observed (i.e., in Figure 2 this equivalent is 23). Have them interpolate their result down the X axis. In Figure 2, this is approximately 75 m^2, or about 30 percent of the total 16x16 m^2 study site. Thus, 75 m^2 is the minimum site needed to ensure that 75 percent of the study site's total species are observed.

4. Answers will depend on observations. In general, if area is increased, more species should be observed. But the rate of further observations falls as the entire community is observed. The number of species observed doesn't increase proportionally with an increase in area.

5. Answers will vary, depending on the observations the class has made. Environmental conditions could account for the difference. Or, if multiple classes are using the same study site, earlier inventories may reduce the number of species as samples are collected.

Part B: Using the Species-Area Equation

1. Students can answer this question by using the species-area equation and plugging in their values for A, c, and z. Have them work with different size reductions in habitat area until they become comfortable with how the species-area equation operates.

2. Climate change, overharvesting certain species to a point where food webs become affected, and water and air pollution are possibilities.

Part C: Applying Data to Preserving Biodiversity

1. Yes, if students assume that their sanctuary is the only place these plants will exist. But something less than 100 percent may be saved in considerably less space.

2. The sidewalk might create an edge effect, which would impact the species residing immediately adjacent to it. As sometimes occurs in large ecosystems, an edge effect could fragment the ecosystem for some species. If wide enough, the sidewalk could interfere with pollination. If heavily trafficked, trash and other disturbances could accumulate.

3. Examples include, but are not limited to: change in climate, change in human use, and the introduction of new or foreign species that could drive out indigenous ones.

Suggestions for Further Study

• In Part A, data analysis represents a critical part of research; without it, observations lose their value. Part A focuses on identifying the minimum area needed to maintain a given number of species in a particular habitat. However, that does not mean that other things can't be learned from the data. Students should, as part of their analysis, identify other potential areas of study for patterns. For example, have them describe the distribution of different kinds of plants found on the study plot. Have them compare the kinds of plants on the study plot with the kinds of plants found nearby in habitats different than the lawn habitat. They can address these areas in future activities once they have completed their main biodiversity data analysis.

• Human ingenuity and technological achievement have done much to help soften the impact of human activity on ecosystems. But the interdependence of living organisms often weaves a web so complex that, despite our best efforts, we are unable to foresee every eventuality. Have students research the attempt to design, build, and operate a self-perpetuating ecosystem, the Biosphere II project. As they conduct their researches, have students consider what they might have done differently, and how such differences might have impacted the project. If time allows, you may want to encourage students to design their own self-perpetuating ecosystems, either individually or in groups. If done in groups, such an exercise can be used to highlight the way that human interaction affects a scientific undertaking. Also, you can suggest to students that they must find ways of funding their "Biosphere" project as a means of highlighting the relationship between financial resources and scientific undertakings.

Becoming an Amateur or "Para" Taxonomist

Objective
To become amateur taxonomists through field collection and species identification.

Background

In this activity, students will acquire some basic skills needed to become amateur taxonomists. Taxonomy, or scientific classification, is the method by which scientists organize and identify living things. Without it, there would be no orderly way to describe the relationships between the millions of species we know to exist—and no way to clearly determine when we have discovered a new species. In order to fully understand how fast biodiversity is disappearing, we first have to be able to estimate how much biodiversity there is. Taxonomy helps answer that question. It is both art and science, although the classification of plants and animals is based on concrete evidence such as biochemical characteristics. Taxonomists sometimes have to make educated guesses based on their observation and their best understanding of the evolutionary relationships among the organisms. Since there aren't enough taxonomists, funds, or time to conclusively study every living species, the science of taxonomy is constantly changing.

Taxonomy is one of the few scientific areas in which both professionals and amateurs can contribute. For example, one of the leading authorities on beetles in the United States is not a professional entomologist, but a retired postmaster. Students with interest and persistence can become experts in a particular species of fauna or flora, and in the process come to better understand biology, ecology, and evolution. Very dedicated amateurs can make solid contributions to the effort to catalog biodiversity.

Figure 1
The most common species of firefly in North America is *Photinus puralis*. There are about 1,900 species of this relative of the beetle, some able to light up and some not, within the family Lampyridae.

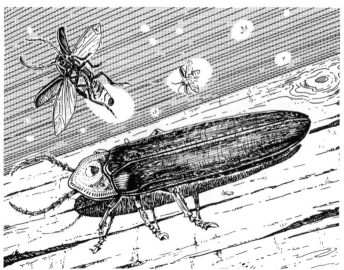

Procedure

1. In class or as homework, have students research species native to your area. Resources include libraries, *Peterson Field Guides*, U.S. Department of Agriculture extension offices, web sites, and taxonomy organizations (see the Resources List on the inside back cover).

2. Divide the class into groups, and have each group select a species of insect or plant to focus on. Plants and insects are suggested because they are common, numerous, and easily collected. Good candidates include beetles (there are 88,600 beetle species in North America alone), ants, butterflies, grasses, and ferns. *Students should not collect samples in protected areas.*

3. Have each group research the species it chose. Before collecting, they should know their choice's scientific name, physical description, habitat, and life cycle. Students should also be familiar with techniques for collection and storage. Field guides and encyclopedias are helpful.

4. Have each group collect samples of their species. For some species, such as the family Lampyridae (Figure 1), collection will have to occur during certain times of day, such as in the evening.

5. To properly identify their species, students will have to perform the following analyses:
   - Where was a sample collected, and under what conditions? If studying an insect, what characterizes its behavior?
   - What are its physical characteristics? Have students use a microscope if necessary. Have them make educated guesses about identification. If a positive identification can't be made, have them identify distinguishing characteristics. Students may also attempt to identify their sample's stage in its life cycle.

6. After students have completed their research and analyses, have each group share with the class what they observed during the collection and identification process. How many different kinds of insect were collected and under what conditions? What criteria were developed to identify a sample to species? Did identification criteria include behavioral as well as physiological characteristics?

7. Ask students to hypothesize how they would know if they had discovered a new species. Ask them how they would go about taxonomically classifying it.

Materials
Peterson Field Guides, or similar nature guides
Jars, zipper-locked bags, petri dishes, or other collecting and storing materials
Dissecting microscope, or 15x magnifying lens

Time Management
If research is assigned as homework, this activity may be completed over 2–3 class periods.

23

Questions for Discussion

1. If students were able to positively identify their sample, is it rare or common in your area?

2. What observations can be made about the role a specimen plays in its particular ecosystem?

3. Ask students why is it important to be able to taxonomically catalog biodiversity?

Answers to Discussion Questions

1. Answer depends on whether student can identify his or her sample.

2. Answers will vary depending on what students collect, but should demonstrate an understanding of the relationship between an organism and its environment. For examples, insects are food for species like birds, reptiles, and small mammals, and may also act as pollinators.

3. It is important to catalog diversity in order to know, in a "snapshot," what lives in an area. Taxonomy and biodiversity studies also provide raw information for economic concerns seeking new solutions for medical problems, new chemicals, etc.

Only 1,413,000 of an estimated 10–100 million species have actually been taxonomically identified. Of that number, more than 751,000 are insects, and about 248,000 are higher plants.

How many species are there?

Type	Known	Undiscovered
Insects	950,000	8–100 million
Algae	40,000	200,000 to 10 million
Bacteria	4,000	400,000 to 3 million
Fungi	70,000	1–1.5 million
Spiders	75,000	750,000 to 1 million
Worms	15,000	500,000 to 1 million
Viruses	5,000	500,000
Plants	250,000	300,000–500,000
Mollusks	70,000	200,000
Protozoa	40,000	100,000–200,000
Crustaceans	40,000	150,000
Vertebrates	45,000	50,000

Suggestions for Further Study

• Students can research the role the U.S.-based pharmaceutical company Merck & Co., Ltd., played in supporting INBio. To begin their research, familiarize them with the relationship between Merck and INBio using the sidebar materials on page 34. Have students address questions such as: Why would a large pharmaceutical company take such a financial risk? Further resources may be found in the Resources List on the inside of the back cover.

• Have students research recent or historical occasions when rare species provided the solution to a medical problem. For example, the Pacific yew provides a component of Taxol™, which is used to treat ovarian cancer. Another example is the rosy periwinkle (see page 34) which has provided the genetic basis for two anti-cancer drugs.

• Have students watch and discuss the film, *Medicine Man*. Encourage them to pay particular attention to the scientific methodology employed by the film's protagonists.

Parataxonomists in Costa Rica

Costa Rica's survey of its biological diversity is an enormous task—and one with limited resources. Because both money and people with Ph.D's in taxonomy are scarce in Costa Rica, the country's National Biodiversity Institute (INBio) turned to an abundant, previously underutilized resource—rural Costa Ricans. Beginning in 1988, INBio trained a group of national park employees in the essential skills needed to conduct the biodiversity survey. In addition to traditional courses such as as ornithology, herpetology, entomology, crytogamic botany, and field botany, INBio students also studied natural history and basic taxonomy. They also learned the more practical aspects of their new career—how to collect, prepare, and transport specimens, how to work in the forest at night, how to use computers and topographic maps, and other aspects of field work. The most successful parataxonomists are independent, self-motivated people who can work alone.

Although they send their samples to INBio for analysis and classification, the parataxonomists are more than collectors. To collect the right kinds and numbers of specimens, INBio parataxonomists must be able to address the following questions:

• How does one use biodiversity information, such as reference collections, habitats and climates, kinds and numbers of species, and locations of species populations, to survey biodiversity? How does such information help in the conservation management of an area?

• How many of a "species" should be collected? How do you decide where to collect? How do you know when it is time to move on?

• How do you determine if a collecting technique is damaging the biota of an area?

• How is a field guide produced, and what information is necessary to collect for it?

• How are scientific names produced? Why do we need them? How can they be used to locate other information? What is a "species"? What is a population?

• What is the basic natural history of the flora and fauna of a given area? How do these histories relate to a biodiversity survey?

INBio parataxonomists also have to understand the many policy issues relevant to park management and conservation. In covering such issues, INBio hopes both to complete the survey of Costa Rica's rich biodiversity and, at the same time, train a cadre of people to value and use this precious natural resource.

Life Zones in Costa Rica

Background

Objective
To understand how factors, such as movements of air masses, topography, temperature, biotemperature, and rainfall, determine environmental conditions.

All three parts of this activity use a simplified version of the Holdridge Classification of World Life Zones, or the Holdridge System. In Part A, students learn how geographical and climatic data interact to define the life zone classifications. In Part B, students interpret data to classify their school's life zone. In Part C, students use the Holdridge System to explore environmental conditions among three locations in Costa Rica.

The Holdridge System was devised by ecologist L. R. Holdridge beginning in the 1940s, and was later tested in Costa Rica and Thailand. The Holdridge System classifies ecosystems according to the effects of temperature (geography) and rainfall (climate) on vegetation. The interaction of these two factors determines what vegetation appears in an ecosystem and how it is distributed within. The life zones are delineated by the convergence of lines originating from points on two axes: average total annual precipitation and mean annual biotemperature (mab).

Other factors also interact to determine environmental conditions, such as the movements of air masses and local and regional topography. As they work through this activity, students will gain an understanding of how Costa Rica's geography and climate interact to determine its environmental conditions, which in turn affect its biodiversity.

Precipitation and Biotemperature

The Holdridge System accords greater weight to average total annual precipitation than it does to monthly precipitation figures. Holdridge found that vegetation type and distribution correspond more directly to annual averages, which are relatively consistent, than it does to the relatively inconsistent patterns of how long or how short a wet or dry season lasts. That's why an average total annual precipitation axis is used instead of a latitudinal axis. For each latitudinal belt, a "normal" precipitation pattern can be described. The same holds true for the average annual biotemperature axis: for each altitudinal belt, a "normal" temperature pattern can be described.

Part A: Understanding Life Zones

Procedure

Have students use the Holdridge Classification of World Life Zones (Figure 2, next page) to address the following:

(Figure 2, next page)

1. Within which degrees latitude are the tropical climates found?

2. What is a term used to describe biotemperatures at 60°–70° North and South latitude?

3. What is the name of a life zone which is temperate, but which has a total of only 4.5 cm of rain in an average year?

4. What life zone has the largest range of annual rainfall?

5. A savanna is a life zone having tall grasses, scattered trees, and large animals, such as giraffes, zebras, hyenas, wildebeests, and lions (Figure 1). Where would the savanna be positioned on the diagram?

6. At least two kinds of forest life zones (other than rain forests) can be identified. One kind loses its leaves during the cold season, and the other kind loses its leaves during the warm season. Suggest more specific names for these life zones, and identify where each would exist on Earth.

7. Which of the lines in the diagram would correspond to the timberline, observed as one goes up a large mountain?

8. What other relationships from this diagram can be applied to the different life zones of a mountain due to altitude?

Figure 1
A sampling of savannah wildlife.

Materials
Holdridge Classification of World Life Zones (Figure 2, page 28)

Time Management
Parts A and B of this activity may be completed in one class period. Part C may be completed in one class period if student research is assigned as homework.

27

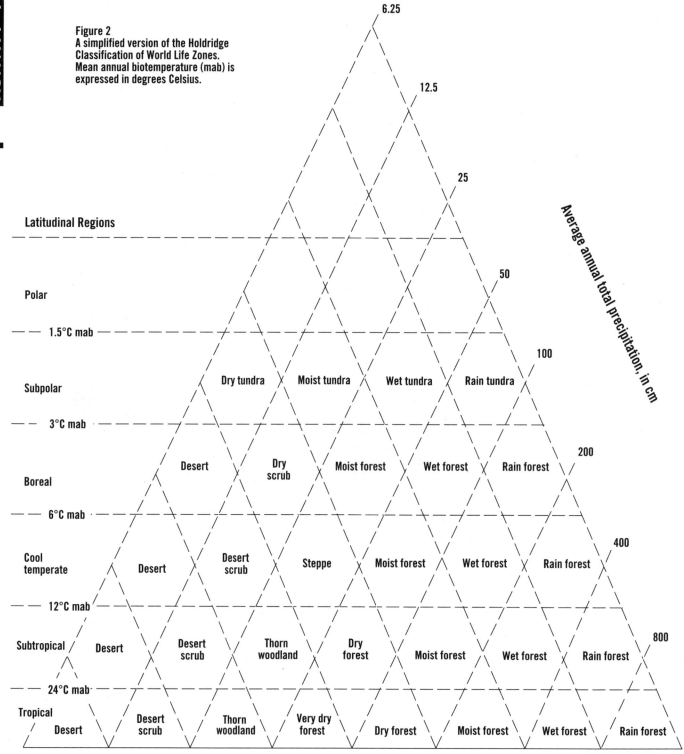

Figure 2
A simplified version of the Holdridge
Classification of World Life Zones.
Mean annual biotemperature (mab) is
expressed in degrees Celsius.

Part B: Classifying Your School's Life Zone

Procedure

1. Have students obtain two data sets for their school's region from the nearest weather station: monthly precipitation and average monthly temperature. Request data for the most recent complete year, and convert them to centimeters and Celsius if necessary.

2. Have students calculate the average total annual precipitation for their school by adding the monthly precipitation figures and dividing by 12. Have them calculate their school's average annual biotemperature by adding the monthly averages and dividing by 12. (If any values appear below 0° or above 30° Celsius, count them as zeros. Vegetation is only physiologically active within a temperature range of 0°–30° Celsius.)

3. Students now have the two points needed to plot their school's life zone on the Holdridge System—average annual total precipitation and mean annual biotemperature. Have students locate the corresponding points on the appropriate axes, and simultaneously trace them inward until they converge. Students may now classify their school's life zone.

4. Using a United States map, have students identify their school's latitude and altitude. A local topographical map, almanac, or atlas may be needed to find local altitude.

5. Using a world map with topographical features, have students identify locations sharing their school's latitude. Ask them if they think those places share the same environmental conditions as their school. If not, why not? Have them pay particular attention to altitudes among the locations they identify. How might altitude affect temperature?

Part C: Classifying Costa Rica's Life Zones

Procedure

1. Before class begins, prepare photocopies for distribution of page 31, which contains Data for Three Locations in Costa Rica (Figure 3), a Topographic Map of Costa Rica (Figure 4), and Atmospheric Effects in Costa Rica (Figure 5).

Materials
Holdridge's Classification of World Life Zones (Figure 2, page 28)
United States topographical map
World topographical map or atlas

Materials
Holdridge's Classification of World Life Zones (Figure 2, page 28)
Data for Three Locations in Costa Rica (Figure 3, page 31)
Topographic Map of Costa Rica (Figure 4, page 31)
Atmospheric Effects in Costa Rica (Figure 5, page 31)

2. Have students use the Data for Three Locations in Costa Rica to classify each location's life zone.

3. Now have students note that each location lies on approximately the same latitude. Have them brainstorm hypotheses about environmental conditions among the three locations. Do they share the same environmental conditions? If not, why not? Do they contain the same species of vegetation? If not, why not? Have students support their hypotheses with data from the Data for Three Locations in Costa Rica table. Encourage them to pay particular attention to precipitation and altitude.

4. Now have students locate the three locations—Limón, San José, and Puntarenas—on the Topographic Map of Costa Rica. Have them pay particular attention to topographical features associated with each location, and revise their hypotheses from Step 3 using the information contained in Atmospheric Effects in Costa Rica.

5. Have students research the three locations—they are all major Costa Rican cities—to learn about their actual environmental conditions. Depending on time and resource availability, this may be assigned as homework for individuals or groups. Research may be conducted using traditional library resources, but electronic sources, such as the World Wide Web, will also be effective.

6. Have students compare and contrast their hypotheses from Steps 3 and 4 with what they have learned from their research.

Why do tropical forests have such great biodiversity?

Scientists define a tropical forest as forest growing in regions with at least 200 cm of annual rainfall spread evenly enough through the year to allow a heavy growth of broad-leaved evergreen trees. Tropical forest is arrayed in multiple layers, from upper canopy 30 m or more in height, broken by scattered emergent trees soaring over 40 m, down through ragged middle levels to chest-high understory shrubs (Figure 6). Contrary to popular portrayals of dense undergrowth that requires a machete for human passage, tropical forests are green cathedrals because of the upper canopy's interception of solar radiation.

The reasons for greater biodiversity in tropical forests remain controversial. One theory, the Energy-Stability-Area Theory (ESA), links three factors: more solar energy means greater standing biomass, more stable climate means more evenly distributed rainfall and more consistent temperatures, and the larger the area means more room for a more diverse variety of species. Whichever theory one prefers, it is a general organizing principle of biology that biodiversity becomes greater as one moves from polar toward equatorial regions. This principle is called the latitudinal diversity gradient.

Name	Latitude	Longitude	Altitude Above Sea Level	Average Annual Biotemperature	Average Annual Precipitation
Puntarenas	09 58N	084 50W	3 m	27° C	1,700 mm
San José	09 56N	094 05W	1,172 m	19° C	1,930 mm
Limón	10 00N	083 02W	3 m	25° C	3,550 mm

Figure 3
Data for Three Locations in Costa Rica. (Data cover the 10-year period, 1971–1980. From the World Meteorological Organization.)

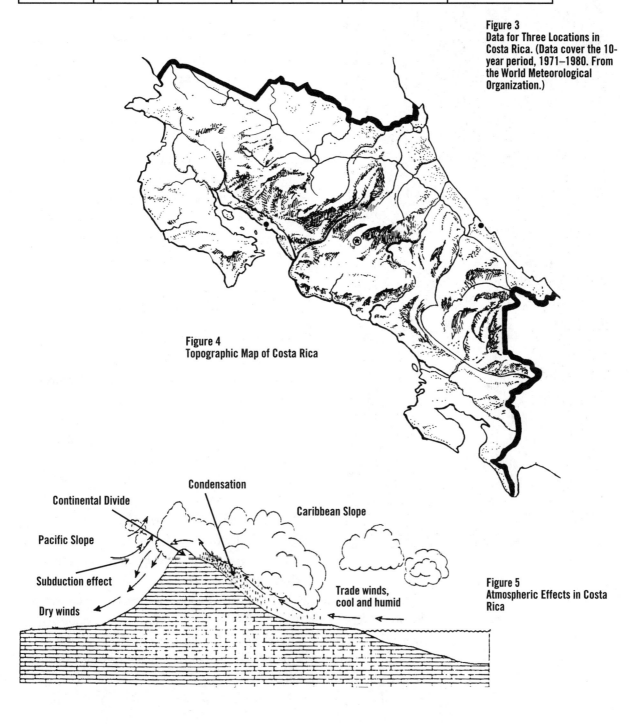

Figure 4
Topographic Map of Costa Rica

Figure 5
Atmospheric Effects in Costa Rica

Summary and Discussion

While rainfall and temperature are considered the main determinants of environmental conditions, such as diversity of biological species, other factors also contribute significantly. It is important for students to understand that ecology involves identifying and understanding interactions among a range of factors. It is equally important for them to appreciate that the impact of human activity on any or all of those interactions is also a significant contributing factor.

Costa Rica exemplifies a particularly unusual range of interactions, due primarily to its dramatic topography and its location on the Central American Isthmus. Costa Rica is so narrow—119 km minimum and 464 km maximum width—that atmospheric disturbances originating in the Caribbean Sea can affect the entire country, not just its eastern coast. The same is true of disturbances originating in the Pacific Ocean. Costa Rica's mountainous central axis is oriented almost perpendicularly to prevailing wind patterns, and can modify weather systems passing over and through.

Suggestions for Further Study

• Part B may be extended beyond having students merely surmise about the differences between their school's environmental conditions and those of locations sharing the same latitude. One such extension is to have students collect actual data about these places from the National Oceanic and Atmospheric Administration (NOAA) Climate Services Division in Ashville, North Carolina; 704-271-4800 (phone); 704-271-4876 (fax). Or collect such data beforehand and have it ready when the class reaches that portion of the activity.

Figure 6
A tropical forest layered canopy.

• Have students research how weather and climatic data are collected. Weather stations are typically located at airports and in developed areas. Have students address how such locations might influence the collected data. For example, developed areas usually have far less vegetation than undeveloped areas, and far more concrete and other types of structures. Might this have a significant effect on the data?

Valuing Biodiversity

Background

In this two-part activity, students will gain an understanding of bio-diversity's value. In Part A, students examine some everyday products and materials derived from a biologically diverse ecosystem, a rain forest, and discuss some of their commercial and practical uses. In Part B, students explore biodiversity's ecological value. Students first investigate the interrelatedness among biological components of a representative food web. They then remove one or several of those components and examine the impact on remaining species.

As you lead students through this activity, encourage them to keep in mind some of the following examples of biodiversity's existing and potential value:

Commercial Value. The value of biodiversity to the pharmaceutical industry is considerable. One in four prescription drugs currently on the market is derived from genetic information found in tropical ecosystems. The National Academy of Science reports that tropical rain forests contain an estimated 70 percent of the 3,000 plant species known to have anti-cancer properties (Figure 1).

Because tropical rain forests have so much biodiversity, they harbor a huge amount of genetic information. Genetic information is used to stabilize food crops, develop stronger construction materials, and hybridize ornamental plants and food products. Perhaps some of your students will invent new and exciting uses for the genetic information found in tropical rain forest biodiversity.

The search for the genetic information contained in tropical rain forests is called biodiversity prospecting. Many business concerns are rushing to collect biological samples they hope will provide the genetic basis for creating new, marketable products. As a result, biodiversity's commercial value is being redefined, and new international markets are being established.

Debt-for-Nature. Many developing nations are burdened by large

Objective
To understand biodiversity's existing and potential value.

Time Management
This activity may be completed in two class periods, if student research and presentation development is assigned as homework.

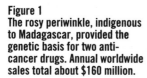

Figure 1
The rosy periwinkle, indigenous to Madagascar, provided the genetic basis for two anti-cancer drugs. Annual worldwide sales total about $160 million.

debts to international lending agencies. During the 1980s, several environmental groups convinced lenders to forgive economic debt in exchange for natural resource preservation, especially rain forests. Called debt-for-nature swaps, such exchanges have redefined the value of rain forest ecosystems.

Ecotourism. Another example of biodiversity's new commercial value is the ecotourism industry. Many people living in places without as much biodiversity, such as Europe, Canada, Japan, and the United States, are eager to travel to places where many biological species coexist in natural habitats. Costa Rica is leading the way in developing this new industry, and its efforts are closely watched by nations containing tropical and other endangered ecosystems.

Ecotourism is not, however, problem free. The sheer numbers of tourists can have a negative impact on an ecosystem. Establishing a model for ecotourism means figuring out how to provide physical access to natural habitats without damaging them. It also means providing local people with a more long-term understanding of a natural habitat's uses. While building a hotel or airport means immediate jobs and a boost to local economies, it can also mean the eventual destruction of the reason for building them in the first place.

Making biodiversity profitable

In 1991, INBio and the U.S.-based pharmaceutical company Merck & Co., Ltd., announced an agreement under which INBio would provide Merck with chemical extracts from wild plants, insects, and microorganisms from Costa Rica's national parks for Merck's drug-screening program. In return, INBio got a two-year research and sampling budget of $1,135,000, as well as royalties on any resulting commercial products. This contract, renewed in 1995, is the first of its kind. It is serving as a model for biodiversity prospecting between organizations performing national biodiversity inventories and pharmaceutical concerns around the world.

As part of its agreement with Merck, INBio contributes 10 percent of its budget and 50 percent of all royalties to Costa Rica's National Parks Fund. Merck also provides on-site technical assistance and training toward establishing laboratory and research facilities in Costa Rica. Biodiversity is becoming an important national asset, just like oil, gas, and minerals. Costa Rica is the first developing nation to parlay this asset into a transfer of funds and advanced technology.

Local Value. Many local populations rely on biodiversity for sustenance. For people who live in and around biologically diverse environments like rain forests, biodiversity is a source of nutrition and shelter (Figure 2). It's important for students to remember that some people value biodiversity for reasons that may have little to do with international economics or the advancement of scientific knowledge.

Ecological Value. Species become interdependent as they develop ecological and biological relationships. As a result of this interrelatedness, the loss of one species can cause the loss of others. Because of their position in the food web as primary producers, the loss of plant species can have a significant impact on other species in an ecosystem.

Biodiversity stabilizes ecosystems and strengthens their ability to recover from environmental change and human disruption. Recent scientific studies have shown that ecosystems ranging from forests to wetlands—even urban lawns—recover faster from drought, disease, and other stresses if they harbor many species rather than just one or a few. The more species an ecosystem contains, the more likely some of them will be resistant to environmental stress.

Inherent Value. Many people think biodiversity is valuable for its own sake, apart from its ability to stabilize ecosystems or provide for human needs. This is a matter of debate, but ethics have played an important role in recent international conferences about how human action is affecting natural environments. Such was the case at the 1992 United Nations Earth Summit in Rio de Janeiro, Brazil, and at the 1995 United Nations Convention on Biological Diversity in Jakarta, Indonesia.

Figure 2
Local people rely on biodiversity for sustenance, providing a value quite apart from international economics and scientific advancement.

Materials
Select items from this list according to availibility and class size.
   Woods
      balsa
      mahogany
      rosewood
      sandalwood
   Fibers
      bamboo
      rattan
   Foods
      avocado
      banana
      grapefruit
      lemon
      lime
      mango
      orange
      papaya
      pineapple
      plantain
      coconut
      coffee
      sugar
      tea
   Spices
      allspice
      black pepper
      cayenne
      chocolate
      cinnamon
      cloves
      ginger
      paprika
      vanilla

Part A: Examining Rain Forest Products and Materials

Procedure

1. Distribute the items derived from the rain forest among students. Depending on the size of your class and the availability of rain forest products in your area, you may want to divide the class into working groups.

2. Have students use library, electronic, and other resources to research and address the following points.

• Describe the type of plant the product or material came from.
• What part of the plant is used to make the material?
• How is it used, by humans, other species, or both?
• How was it discovered?
• Where in the rain forest is it to be found?
• Are there substitutes, such as synthetic alternatives?
• What is the commercial value of their product or material?
• What is the practical value of their product or material?

3. Have students develop short presentations to share their findings with their classmates. This may be done as homework. After students have made their presentations, lead a class discussion comparing and contrasting the various student findings.

Figure 3
Many everyday products, such as these cacao pods from which cocoa is made, come from tropical forests.

Part B: Exploring Biodiversity's Ecological Value

Procedure

1. Divide the class into four groups, and have each group recreate the representative food web from Figure 4 on one of the large poster boards. This food web provides a simplified representation of trophic relationships among biological species inhabiting the southern tip of Costa Rica's Nicoya Peninsula (Figure 5).

2. Have students assign their food web's biological components to one of three trophic levels—producers (green plants), herbivores (plant eaters), and carnivores (meat eaters).

3. Have each group remove a biological component from its food web by pasting a white piece of paper over it on the poster board. Each group should remove a species from a different trophic level, i.e., one group removes a primary producer, another group an herbivore, and so forth.

4. Have each group examine its altered food web and determine the impact of the species' removal on the web's other species.

5. Once the groups have agreed upon how their food web has been altered by the species' removal, have all the groups compare and contrast their findings in a general class discussion. As you lead the discussion, encourage students to realize that the removal of even a single species from one trophic level can have an impact on more than one species among all trophic levels.

Materials
Four large poster boards
Magic markers in assorted colors
Representative food web

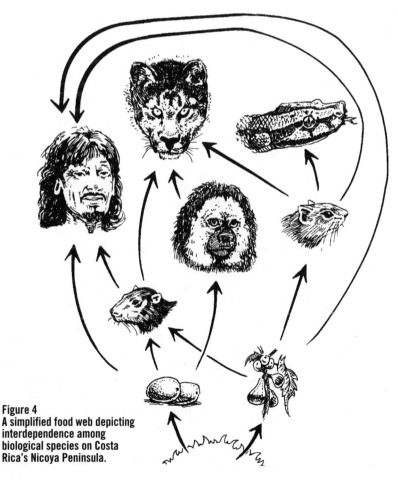

Figure 4
A simplified food web depicting interdependence among biological species on Costa Rica's Nicoya Peninsula.

Figure 5
Geographic location of Costa Rica's Nicoya Peninsula.

What is a keystone species?

All species within a community are important, but a keystone species (or group of species) is one that plays an especially large role in a community's structure or processes. A keystone species may be a major predator who limits the abundance of prey, therefore reducing competition between the prey species. Another keystone species might be a unique food source, such as figs and palms that bear fruit during seasons of fruit scarcity. Another example would be a species that maintains critical ecosystem processes, such as nitrogen-fixing bacteria or phosphorous-mobilizing fungi. Removing a keystone species can impact the entire community by leaving other members of the community vulnerable to extinction. The links between keystone species and their communities are critical in tropical forests, which are highly interdependent.

Questions for Discussion
Part A

1. What roles do humans play in the food web? What would happen if humans were removed from that web?

2. Can you identify the types of keystone species (plant or animal) that are important in a tropical forest?

3. Do you think partnerships, such as the one between INBio and Merck, are effective? Why or why not?

Why does biodiversity matter?

Biodiversity describes three fundamental categories of life on Earth: genetic diversity, species diversity, and ecosystem diversity. Genetic diversity refers both to the differences in genetic make-up among distinct species and to the genetic variations within a single species. The gene pool is the sum total of all the genes and all the various potential combinations those genes represent. Far more genetic variation is possible (10^{600}) than can ever be expressed among the individual organisms alive at a given time.

Biodiversity matters for many reasons, such as its ability to stabilize ecosystems and to strengthen their ability to recover from damage. But perhaps the most crucial reason that biodiversity matters is the potential represented by the gene pool. Human activity is placing artificial limits on this potential by removing some species' genetic contribution, and many scientists think this may cause the greatest long-term harm to Earth's overall ecological health. Extinction not only removes a species from its stabilizing role in an ecosystem's energy flow, but it also removes any potential genetic contribution that a species might make after an as yet unforseen major environmental change.

Part B

1. Removing a single species from the repesentative food web had an impact on remaining species within the food web. If the remaining species are unable to adapt to this change by finding new places to live and new sources of nutrition in their existing environment, what might happen to them?

2. Students thought of actual reasons why species might be removed from a food web. Among the reasons they cited, do any of them result in the removal of only one species at a time, as might occur through overhunting?

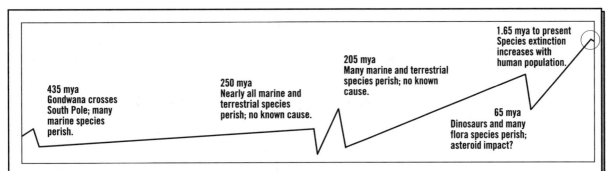

Figure 6
A stylized timeline of Earth's major extinction episodes. Gradual, upward trends indicate the evolution of diverse species over time, while downward trends indicate an extinction episode. Major extinction episodes are not thought to have eradicated large numbers of species all at once, but instead precipitated environmental changes that led to species extinctions over time. The downward trend at the far right denotes the onset of a new extinction episode, caused in large part by habitat loss. Studying the fossil record enables scientists to develop a means of comparing the current rate of species extinction with rates of species extinction in Earth's geologic history.

What are mass extinctions?

One central question in paleontology and biology is whether species are inherently susceptible to extinction at any time, or whether they are threatened only by short periods of extreme stress—such as climate change or habitat destruction. Studying Earth's fossil record can help determine if the extinctions now occurring are "normal" or, as many suspect, represent a new pattern of major extinction.

Throughout Earth's history, there have been times of great diversity interspersed with periods of mass extinction. Global climate change and other, more sudden environmental changes likely caused such mass extinctions. At least two major extinctions essentially rearranged the order of life, favoring some biological groups and changing the evolutionary path of others. The first one we have good fossil records for occurred 250 million years ago at the end of the Paleozoic Era, taking 77–96 percent of Earth's species. The second took place 65 million years ago at the end of the Mesozoic Era, taking at least half of all species, including dinosaurs. After each of these extinctions, diversity recovered slowly over millions of years. The end of the dinosaurs ushered in the current period, which has greater species diversity than ever before.

Between these two major extinctions, several smaller extinctions occurred. But for the most part, the fossil record points to periods of biological stability lasting as long as hundreds of thousands of years. The fossil record offers the best clues as to what a "normal" rate of extinction is. The average extinction rate for the entire history of life has until recently amounted to about two per year in a biosphere containing two million species.

3. Some of the students' reasons might have included a cataclysmic event, like a meteor, earthquake, or volcano. While it's true that such an event can lead to the extinction of one or even many species, students should understand that such events don't cause extinction all at once. They do cause large-scale, sometimes global, environmental changes that lead to species extinction and increased rates of species extinction.

3. Ask students if they can identify any other kinds of circumstances that might result in the removal of many biological species from an ecosystem. Are there any human activities that might cause a mass removal or extinction of species? Have students list as many circumstances as possible.

4. Based on what they've learned about the interdependence of biological species and the interrelatedness of ecosystems, ask students what the global environmental impact of such human actions might be.

Answers to Discussion Questions
Part A

1. Humans are a top predator species. Student answers about humans' impact on the food web will vary, but should reflect understanding of the numerous ways humans interact with other parts of the food web.

2. Students will likely be unable to discuss specific keystone species of tropical forests without research. They should, however, understand why these species are critical. For example, one predator species can influence a number of prey species, and a single species may be a crucial food source for a great number of species. Removing only a few important threads of an interdependent forest community can damage the fabric from top to bottom.

3. Answers will vary, but should assess both the economic and environmental importance of such partnerships.

Part B

1. Remaining species might be forced to emigrate to another ecosystem in search of nutrients and shelter, which could in turn have an effect on species already living there. Students should realize that ecosystems are interrelated through species migration and emigration, and by natural conduits such as wind and hydrological cycling. Species loss in one ecosystem can effect species in ecosystems sometimes far removed. Another possibility for species unable to adapt to such an environmental change is that they could become extinct.

2. Natural events, such as blights and viruses, can and do eliminate a single species from an ecosystem. Human activity, especially large-scale hunting, also results in the removal and outright extinction of a single species, such as the passenger pigeon in the early 1900s. But the more common occurrence is an increase in the rate of species extinction over time, rather than the eradication of a single species.

3. Losing many species can have an impact not only on surrounding ecosystems, but on ecosystems throughout the world. To address this question, have students research Earth's five mass extinction events. Have them compare and contrast species loss among those historic extinction events (Figure 6) with current and projected rates of species loss due to human activity. Currently, the primary cause of species extinction is habitat destruction through human activity.

4. As discussed in activity 2, some scientists point to the current, human-caused rate of species extinction as constituting Earth's sixth mass extinction event. They predict that the repercussions of this rate of species loss won't be fully understood for several, perhaps many, generations.

Suggestions for Further Study

• Orally-transmitted lore among indigenous cultures serves as a source of information for identifying not only the uses to which biological species may be put, but in many cases their very existence. Have students research indigenous peoples, such as those living in rain forests, and their cultures. Have students develop presentations on the impact of non-native peoples, such as European colonialists, on indigenous cultures. Students can then identify and discuss current efforts to protect native peoples and cultures.

• Part B of this activity may be modified in a variety of ways. For example, students can remove various different groupings of species in various different orders and keep a record of the repercussions throughout the food web of each removal. Students can research actual causes of species loss, such as habitat destruction, and remove actual species from actual food webs. Have them compile and collate data about the impact species loss has on existing ecosystems. One effective means of summarizing this suggestion for further study is to have students draw "before-and-after" food webs on large poster boards and display them in the classroom.

Tropical Forest for Sale!

Background

Save tropical forests! We hear this phrase often, but the question is: how do we do this effectively? Preserving tropical forests is a complex task. Simply designating an area "protected" is insufficient. The reasons forests are cut, burned, and otherwise utilized need to be better understood if we are to find workable, long-term solutions. International interests, national laws, economics, scientific knowledge, and local cultures and needs influence all proposed options. Each of these factors must be considered when deciding how to protect forest resources.

How might this be done? Curú National Wildlife Refuge and Farm in Costa Rica, the setting for this activity, provides an example of the conflicts and choices people face when trying to protect a tropical forest. Curú is a real place, privately owned and operated, with 70% of the property managed as natural ecosystems. The current owners developed their own innovative, integrated approach to protection and management. They support the refuge financially through agriculture, cattle ranching, and ecotourism, and they work directly with local communities to try to relieve tensions created by conflicting demands. Their approach is not perfect, and it changes continually.

In this role-playing activity, students will decide for themselves how to juggle the social, political, economic, ecological, and personal problems they encounter. They will learn about the human pressures on tropical forests, evaluate options from different perspectives, and identify the pros and cons associated with each. The roles students will assume are based on actual people, and the situations they will face are real. The places they will learn about can be located on any map of Costa Rica, and read about in guide books.

Objective
To teach students about the complexity of protecting and managing a tropical forest.

Time Management
This activity may be completed in seven, 45–60 minute class periods, extendible to 2–3 weeks. There are four parts to this activity:
  Part A: Introduction (Day 1)
  Part B: Planning (Days 2–5)
  Part C: Presentations
   (Days 6–7)
  Part D: Questions for
   Discussion (Day 7)

Procedure

Before beginning this activity, photocopy the following materials for distribution among the student groups. This distribution scheme assumes a class size of 20 students.

6 copies of the Costa Rica Laws and Decrees (pages 49–51)

6 copies of the Information Packet (pages 52–57)

1 copy each of the student roles in groups A–E (pages 58–62)

5 copies of group F, the legal experts (page 63)

5 copies of group G, the owners (page 63)

5 copies of the Certificate of Legal and Financial Viability (page 64)

Materials
Previous activities
Large paper sheets
Felt markers
Costa Rica Laws and Decrees
 (pages 49–51)
Student Information Packet
 (pages 52–57)
Student roles in groups A–G
 (pages 58–63)
Certificate of Legal and
 Financial Viability (page 64)

Part A: Introduction (Day 1)

1. Tell students they are about to begin an extended project concerning tropical forests. Tell them they will be integrating knowledge and skills from previous activities, as well as from other sources, toward developing a proposal to buy a piece of tropical forest in Costa Rica. Students will play roles, which means they must approach this activity from a viewpoint that may not agree with their own. While they are to play the part as described, students may add to it in any way they feel is appropriate (including dressing the part!). They will work in groups to design the best proposal. One group, the owners, will decide to whom to sell the property.

2. Five groups (A–E) will develop proposals, so distribute their roles as shown in Figure 1. A sixth group (F) will be "legal experts." Legal experts will later assume role G, the "owners." There must be as many individual "legal experts" as there are proposal groups (i.e., 5 legal experts for 5 groups).

Figure 1 (below)
Role distribution scheme. If you have fewer than 15 students, it's better to eliminate an entire group, such as group E, than to eliminate a role from each group. Make sure there is a legal expert (group F; they will also play the owners) assigned to each group. Legal expert roles may require students with good analytical skills who like a challenge.

A: Agriculture	B: Landless People	C: Development	D: Conservation	E: Forestry
1. Cattle rancher	1. Campesino leader	1. Resort developer	1. Forest conservancy vice president	1. Investment manager
2. Agricultural researcher	2. Day laborer	2. Paquera business assn. president	2. ASCONA member	2. Logging company owner
3. Day laborer	3. JUNAFORCA organizer	3. Valle Azul mother	3. Paquera schoolteacher	3. Forest manager

3. Have students read the roles, either in class or as homework.

4. Tell students they should now assume their new identities, and adopt the perspective of their particular characters. Explain the purpose of the activity as follows. Curú Forest and Farm (note that Curú is not a wildlife refuge for this activity) is a 1,500 hectare parcel of land, and it has been put up for sale by the Schutt-Valle family. Each student is now a person with an interest in what happens to the property. Some want to buy it, some want access to its natural resources, and some want to help determine how others use its resources. Soon, students will be assigned to groups, and they must then work together to develop a proposal for buying Curú.

Tell students they must design a proposal outlining: (1) why they want to purchase Curú; (2) how they're going to pay for it; (3) what they intend to do with it; (4) who will take care of it; and (5) whether their proposal is legal according to the Costa Rica Laws and Decrees.

5. Assign students to their groups, and have them introduce and describe themselves according to the roles they've assumed. Encourage students to create names for themselves, as well as for their groups.

6. Distribute an Information Packet to each group. Tell the groups they may use the information it contains in any way they wish. They may not find all of it relevant, or they may want information it doesn't contain. Encourage them to seek out supplemental information according to their perceived needs.

7. Tell each group to begin developing their proposals, which they will be presenting to the "owners" in several days.

8. Give each legal expert (role F) a copy of the Costa Rica Laws and Decrees. Have them read the laws together, discuss their meaning, and agree on their interpretation in the context of this activity. Each legal expert may also be given a copy of the Curú map.

The legal expert group should develop a checklist for reviewing proposals. If possible, help them arrive at this conclusion on their own. Tell them that each legal expert will consult with a purchasing group once the proposals have been designed. If the proposals they encounter have any illegalities, they will need to be able to identify them *and* explain how they might be corrected. This process is outlined for them in their role description.

Part B: Planning (Days 2–5)

1. Groups continue meeting, researching, and discussing. At the beginning of Day 3, each group should informally present its proposal to a legal expert. Assign a legal expert to each group, and instruct them to review their group's proposal. If they identify an illegality, they must suggest an alternative. If everything is legal, have them sign off on a Certificate of Legal and Financial Viability (page 64) for their group. If changes are necessary, the group must rework their proposal with their legal expert. For younger students, two or three legal experts may work together as a consulting team.

2. Also on Day 3 and 4, have each group meet with their "financial advisor" (the teacher) to show how they plan to finance their proposal. Use your own discretion to decide how much detail to require. Each group must, however, demonstrate that they have an understanding of how much their proposal might cost (bid price) and from where they might get financing.

   The group that will have the most trouble acquiring financing is B, the Landless People's group; other groups usually qualify for bank loans. The financial advisor must sign off on the Certificate of Legal and Financial Viability only if the proposal is acceptable. Financial information is contained in the Information Packet, but additional information may be obtained through student research.

3. On Day 5, assuming all necessary signatures have been acquired, have the groups prepare for their formal presentations to the owners. (See Procedure Step 4 for the legal experts' role at this time.) They may represent their proposals in map form on large sheets of paper, or using another format if desired, such as a poster board or 3-D model.

   The owners can sell to whomever they want, so each group's proposal must be persuasive. As indicated in their role description, the owners have a strong personal as well as financial investment in Curú. They understand the importance of science in caring for the land, in making it productive, and in conserving its natural resources while expanding its potential. They also understand that science is one tool among many, and that science tools need to be appropriately integrated with tools from other disciplines to achieve the best results.

   Encourage the groups, therefore, to use scientific data to support their proposals, especially regarding ecological impacts. They should incorporate the knowledge they have acquired from preceding activities, as well as from other sources, into their proposals. Also encourage them to demonstrate an understanding of how to integrate scientific data with information derived from other sources, especially regarding the social and economic impacts of their proposals. Give each group 5–10 minutes for presentation; they should practice beforehand. The signed Certificate of Legal and Financial Viability must be attached to each proposal.

Each group also needs to consider and anticipate what other groups might say to try to discredit and block their proposal, as well as how they might counter any accusations. Groups may want to prepare a pros-and-cons chart to work through such questions.

4. On Day 5 (or whenever their job ends), the legal experts should assume the owners' roles. Each "owner" should select a role as described within the Schutt-Valle family. Have the family create a list of priorities for the sale and agree on some terms. They may use what they learned as legal experts to set their priorities.

Part C: Presentations (Day 6–7)

1. If possible, arrange the classroom into a meeting format, with general seating, a presentation area, and a front table for the owners.

2. Each group is allotted 5–10 minutes to present their proposal, without interruption (presentation order may be determined by lottery). Have the other groups take notes so they can challenge competitors' proposals.

3. Have the owners take notes on proposals and briefly question each group after its presentation.

4. After all presentations are finished, owners and other groups may question individual proposals. Limit the number of questions to between 1 and 3 per challenger group, and request that the questions remain at a "professional" level.

5. Allow the owners 10–15 minutes to discuss and vote on a proposal.

6. Have the owners present their decision and justify their choice.

Part D: Questions for Discussion (Day 7)

This is a chance for students to reflect on the activity. Have them examine their actions as played in character, and compare and contrast those actions with their previously held beliefs and values. What differences and similarities can they identify? Have them discuss the activity's outcome, paying particular attention to the implications of the result. The following questions are for use in a class discussion:

1. Tell students to leave their roles behind. Ask them how they feel about the activity. What happened? Why did it happen the way it did? Do they agree with what happened?

2. What will be the impact of the chosen proposal (ecologically, socially, politically, economically)? What actions could "losing" groups take if they were dissatisfied with the outcome?

3. Different roles are grouped together in this game for a reason. Ask students if they can identify any similarities between the roles in each group. Do they think they would normally work together? If so, how?

4. Ask students what they would do differently if they performed the activity again? What have they learned from their experience?

5. Ask students to connect what they have learned from this activity to another current event they are familiar with. Ask them to think about the applications of the issues they addressed in this activity to other domestic or international situations.

7. Ask students if they liked the activity, and how it can be improved.

Answers to Discussion Questions

There is no preferred or predictable outcome, so there are no right or wrong answers. For assessment, some suggested guidelines follow:

• Before the activity, ask students what they would personally do with a tropical forest if they owned one. Have them explain the reasons for their answers, perhaps in written form. After the activity, ask them the same question. Assess how students use what they have learned to support or alter their original positions.

• Have students write out their responses to the Questions for Discussion to assess their reactions on an individual basis, as well as their ability to express themselves and communicate their ideas.

• Assess each group's ability to work together, the quality of their research and presentation, and the care and consideration they exhibit during their decision-making process.

• Print copies of the criteria established by the legal experts, and give each group a copy. When experts review proposals, have them use this as a checklist of items to approve before signing the certificate.

• Require groups to hand in written pre-proposals at the end of Day 2 and Day 4. Older students may hand in final written proposals.

• Ask Owners to hand in their priorities for selling the land before the presentations. Require written justification for the final decision.

• Encourage students to critically analyze the needs of the various characters, as well as their own views on both this experience and on human use of natural resources in general.

Suggestions for Further Study

Following are suggested variations for altering the activity's dynamics. You may want to collect student suggestions for altering and improving the activity upon completion to derive your own variations in the future.

• Allow students to choose roles instead of assigning them, or assign roles randomly. Assign roles according to predetermined criteria such as personalities, political views, or pre-game assessments.

• Have the groups create a financial plan for their proposals describing expenditures, income sources, capital needed, loan repayment method.

• Allow greater latitude in group presentations, such as videos and computer models, or allot more time for developing written proposals and presentations. Students may want to put greater energy into creating posters or models, or create visuals to scale.

• Have students research the history of land use and distribution in Latin America. Compare Latin America's colonization by Europeans with that of the United States and Canada, and contrast the impacts of each on indigenous populations.

• Students with roles pertaining to ecotourism can conduct marketing surveys; other students may be "tourists." Have student "journalists" interview characters as the activity unfolds, and perform news "reports."

• Students can investigate foundations that provide grants for forest preservation, agricultural assistance, and natural resource development. The Foundations section in the Information Packet (Table 4) provides a starting point. What types of projects will such foundations allow, and how much money will they provide?

Costa Rica's Environmental Laws and Decrees

Forests

A. Forestry Law of 1986: All mangrove forests are declared forest reserves (see Protected Wild Area classifications).

B. Emergency Decree of September 18, 1987:
- The National Forest Service must determine the remaining hectares of forest and develop a management plan for its protection.
- Reduce the number of logging concessions and cutting permits.
- Cut no tree without a government permit, even on private land.
- Bank credits for the expansion of livestock and other agricultural activities that lead to the removal of forest are prohibited.
- *IDA—Instituto para el Desarrollo Agrario* (Institute for Agrarian Development) must set aside 10% of the land under its jurisdiction for forest development.
- All unfinished forest products are banned from export.

C. Forestry Law of 1990: Provides the following incentives for forest management and reforestation:
1) property tax exemption for registered lands.
2) tax exemption on reforestation machinery brought into the country.
3) elimination of income tax on plantation-harvested wood.
4) government protection against *precarista* (illegal squatters) invasion.

A forest management plan must be approved by the National Forest Service in order to qualify. Management plans must include: a physical description of the area (both geological and ecological), a silvicultural description (species lists, tree cropping practices), economic analysis, infrastructure to be constructed, and machinery to be used.

D. Forest Service Mandate: All land owners must protect a strip of forested land 200 m on either side of mountain water sources, or 100 m on either side if waters originate in the plains. A 50 m band of trees must protect along borders with steep slopes. A 10 m band must protect watersheds along flat riverbanks.

Agriculture

A. *FODEA—Fomentacion del Desarrollo Agropecuario* (Promotion of Agriculture and Livestock Development)
- Provides credit for agricultural land owners.
- Farmers without land title may use cattle as collateral for mortages.
- Provides loan refinancing for cattle farmers.

B. *Programa Desarrollo Campesino 1986* (Campesino Development Program) provides peasant farmers with money for agriculture and reforestation projects. To qualify one must:
1) belong to a registered organization or cooperative.
2) live on the farm in question and use it as a primary income source.

3) have a yearly gross income less than 900,000 colones.

4) reforest 1–5 hectares per year for five years.

5) have title to the land.

6) submit a management plan including how technical assistance of the cooperative, organization, or the National Forestry Service is needed.

C. *Precarista* Rights

Individuals living on land to which they do not hold title (do not own) for 10 years may claim it as their own. This does not apply to individuals paid to work for the owner of the land during those 10 years. After 10 years, individuals may register the land in their name if they bring witnesses to testify the land was occupied during said period.

Conservation

A. The National Conservation Strategy:

1) To consolidate and manage the wild areas of Costa Rica.

2) To educate the public of their responsibilities to make decisions about the use of the environment and natural resources, and the importance of conservation and rational use of resources.

B. *MIRENEM—Ministerio de Recursos Naturales, Energia y Minas* (Ministry of Natural Resources, Energy and Mines) may take private lands if deemed valuable and declare such lands as Protected Wild Areas under the following classifications:

1) *Reservas Forestales* (Forest Reserves) are zones formed in forests with the principal function of wood production. This zone must be on such land as is appropriate for that purpose. Zones should be large enough for wood production, water protection, forage, wildlife, and/or recreation. These may be called National Forests.

2) *Zonas Protectoras* (Protected Zones) are areas with forests or containing forestable lands with the principal function of soil protection and watershed preservation. These most often occur at the tops of hills and mountains. The zones' sizes are not as important as is the protection of soil and water.

3) *Parques Nacionales* (National Parks) are areas established to protect and conserve areas containing beautiful natural areas with flora and fauna of national importance. Parks are placed under official vigilance in order that the public may better enjoy them. These areas present one or more ecosystems "untouched" or little changed by humans. Plant and animal species, geomorphological sites, species of special scientific interest, areas with practical recreational or educational value, or areas with natural scenic beauty are considered for this classification. The area must be extensive, on unaltered land, and be able to be maintained in a wild state.

3a) *Refugios Nacionales de Vida Silvestre* (National Wildlife Refuges) are formed for those forests or lands where the principal use is protection, conservation, and management of wild plant and animal species. The area is not necessarily in its "natural state," and its size depends on the needs of the particular habitat.

4) *Reservas Biológicas* (Biological Reserves) are formed in those forests or forested lands whose principal use is conservation and scientific investigation of wildlife and its ecosystems. These should be relatively untouched by humans and should remain so after designation.

Upon declaring a parcel of land a reserve or national park, the government of Costa Rica is legally obliged to: (1) purchase the lands of those occupants who have title, and (2) compensate untitled occupants for "improvements" to land, such as clearing.

C. *Ley sobre la Zona Maritimo Terrestre de 1977* (Law on the Marine and Terrestrial Zone):
- Regulates development and land-use planning in coastal zones.
- Designates a 200 m wide marine and terrestrial zone inland from the ocean's high tide line. These 200 m are divided into a 50 m public zone devoted to public access with private ownership. Development is prohibited. The remaining 150 m of restricted zone are regulated by a concession and permit system based on a detailed plan designed at the county level of local government.
- Marine and Terrestrial Zone property owned before the declaration of this law is exempt from the above ruling.

Legal Points to Consider

Are mangroves properly protected?

Will wood be extracted? If so, have permits been considered? Will wood be used properly?

Are watersheds and rivers properly protected?

Will there be construction along the beach? If so, does it follow the proper guidelines?

Does this proposal qualify for: The Forestry Law of 1990? *FODEA* (Promotion of Agriculture and Livestock Development)? The Campesino Development Program of 1986? If so, explain the necessary qualifications.

Curú's History

Curú is in Northwestern Costa Rica, along the Pacific Ocean, on the southern tip of the Nicoya Peninsula. The name *Curú* comes from the native word for the indigenous pochote tree. Curú is large, with 1,496 hectares of tropical forest, beach, and farmland.

When Don Federico Schutt bought Curú in 1932, its hillsides were barren because all the trees had been cut for timber. He replanted with tropical dry and tropical moist forests. He also planted bananas on Curú's flat areas, which were shipped by boat out to Puntarenas and on to the United States and Nicaragua. But the banana plantation failed because of a soil-borne disease. Don Federico also ran a small logging operation, and he planted teak for harvesting when they became full grown.

The family had to change from bananas, and now they herd beef cattle, sell timber, and grow mangoes, papaya, melon, and coconuts. They also cut a trail system through the forest for tourists, and charge an entrance fee to help protect it. The family has had conflicts with local people, because many want access to Curú for timber, firewood, hunting, and recreation. In 1974, a group of *precaristas*, or squatters, cleared some forest and built homes without permission. The Schutt-Valles asked the government to move them, but it was found that they didn't own the land where the people had settled. The settlement has become the town of Valle Azul (Bye-ay ah-Sool). The family now hires guards to protect the forest, but they also work with local communities to educate people about why the forest is important. Relations have improved between Curú and local communities.

Facts and Figures
Costa Rica

Size: 50,700 square kilometers, about the size of West Virginia.

Human population in 1989: 2,922,372

Currency: dollars to colones (¢), based on 1994 conversion rate: $1.00 U.S. = ¢150

Real estate: The price of land in Costa Rica has skyrocketed. As of late 1994, a square meter of land near Flamingo Beach, an upscale resort community in the northwest province of Guanacaste, sold for $150 U.S. From coastal areas to the central valley, the boom in the Costa Rican real estate market is the direct result of huge increases in tourism. An estimated 700,000 international tourists visited Costa Rica in 1994, and some bought land for their own use or as an investment. In Escazu, a square meter brought as much as $350 U.S., and about $120 U.S. in Jaco. If the right property is purchased—beachfront appreciates more than agricultural land, for example—as much as 400–500 percent can be realized on an investment in real estate. San Jose's leading English-language newspaper, *The Tico Times*, provides frequent updates on developments in Costa Rica's real estate market. The World Wide Web address for *The Tico Times* is http://infoweb.magi.com/calypso/ttimes.html/

Nicoya Peninsula

Length: 100 km

Climate: 1.75–3.0 meters of rain/year, mostly during the rainy season from June through November; hurricane-force winds common during rainy season; little rainfall from December to May; temperatures range from 15–39°C.

Soil: Type II land, capable of moderate production. Low, flat areas have well-drained alluvial soils. Steeply sloped areas have deeply eroded and/or very shallow soils.

Agriculture: Planting and harvesting occurs during the rainy season. Most agricultural labor is hired between May and December, with little work available from January through April. High quantities of corn, rice, and beans are produced and sold on the Peninsula. The typical small farm grows a combination of banana, plantain, papaya, citrus fruits, cassava, corn, beans, and watermelon. Pigs and chickens usually supplement farmer income and diet.

Ranching: Much of the Peninsula is used for cattle grazing, especially the *Brahman* species, *Bos indicus.* Meat and milk products are sold. Typically, ranchers have 0.8 head of cattle per hectare of grazing land. It normally takes about four years for beef cattle to mature to 450 kg.

Curú

Agriculture: 10.5 hectares in mango plantation, 32 hectares in coconut, and 10 hectares in papaya, all for income generation. The remaining agricultural land is a mixture of avocado, banana, guanabana, citrus fruits (oranges and limes), and vegetables for consumption on the property.

Ranching: 285 hectares are in cattle production. Animals are rotated between pastures, where about 430 cattle graze. In 1992, 44,780 kg of meat were produced. Eight years ago, Curú started an artificial insemination program to increase meat production. *Brahmans* sp. were crossed with *Simmental* sp. This increased the rate at which the cattle reached maturity. The genetic improvement means animals reach 480 kg in 26 months.

Forestry: 1,085 hectares of Curú are forested. Eighty hectares were planted in 1970 with teak with plans for future timber extraction. Four years ago, they began replanting the hillsides with eight native and two introduced tree species.

Ecotourism: The number of tourists annually visiting Curú has risen from 825 in 1985 to 2,332 visitors at present. Tourists can hike through the forest, or swim or snorkel in the bay. Curú spends 27% of all expenditures on ecotourism. Income from tourism is increasing. They currently charge $5 a day to visit. They also have seven guest houses, with beds for 2–8 people. Lodging is $30 per night, including meals.

Table 1
Average monthly salaries in Costa Rica (in colones).

Artisan	40,000
Agricultural laborer	28,000
Business owner	41,000–105,000 (varies by type and location)
Doctor	140,000
Government employee	68,000
INBio parataxonomist	50,000
Professional or technical employee	85,000
Rancher	80,000
Service worker	32,000
Average Costa Rican	46,000

Table 2
Percentage of Curú's income
from various sources.

	1988	1989	1990	1991	1992	1993
Produce	9.22	24.76	4.94	8.37	14.99	6.75
Cattle	89.81	71.88	72.83	60.05	38.75	34.81
Ecotourism	.97	3.35	22.23	24.18	37.48	52.77
Timber	—	—	—	7.4	8.77	5.67
Total Income	34,537	73,503	77,217	70,750	113,537	106,210

54

Table 3
Sample wages (in colones)
paid to Curú workers.

Position	Wage/hour	Hours/week	Months/year
Cook	180	30	6
Day laborer	150	45	8
Guard	230	45	12

Table 4
Types of international foundations and
grants available for funding of proposals.

Foundation (Fdtn) Name	Description	Amount Awarded/Grant
Aleman Fdtn for International Development (Berlin, Germany)	Provides information to technical experts, organizes educational programs, produces teaching materials.	$10,000–700,000 average $500,000
Belgian Development Fdtn (Brussels, Belgium)	Provides assistance to rural organizations in developing countries for agricultural, technical, water, and sanitation projects	$1,000–15,000
Between the Americas Fdtn (San Francisco, CA)	Awards for small enterprise development, education, and training; also for small-scale food production and agriculture. No money for land purchases.	$25,000–300,000 average $100,000 over a 3-year-period
The Forest Conservancy (Madison, WI)	Purchases forested lands for protection purposes. Conservancy often keeps the land or donates it to governments for management.	amount highly variable, average purchase $345,000
Fdtn for Environment and Agriculture (Lembruch, Germany)	Promotes research in agricultural practices which help conserve natural resources.	maximum award $50,000
Grace Charitable Trust (New York, NY)	Awards for environmental programs, education, health, and human services. No money for land purchases.	$30,000–300,000
Kloge Fdtn (Lansing, MI)	Awards for leadership training and rural development; also to schools for agricultural training.	$50,000–400,000
Netherlands Fdtn for International Development Cooperation (Amsterdam, Netherlands)	Gives financial and/or technical support to improve the condition of economically deprived groups in developing countries.	$20,000–750,000 average $350,000
Weethen Fdtn (New York, NY)	Purchases land for conservation and protection purposes.	$10,000–30,000

Spanish Name	Latin Name	English Name
araña de oro	*Nephila clavipes*	golden orb-web spider
boa	*Boa constrictor*	boa constrictor
congrejo fantasma	*Ocypode quadrata*	ghost crab
cascabel	*Crotalus durissus*	tropical rattlesnake
caucel	*Felis wiedii*	margay
cherenga	*Dayprocta punctata*	agouti
chiza	*Sciurus variegatoides*	squirrel
comejenes	*Nasitutermes*	termites
coral	*Micrurus nigrocintus*	coral snake
culebra del mar	*Pelamis platurua*	sea snake
gallego	*Basiliscus narica*	basilisk
garrobo	*Ctenosaura similis*	ctenosaur
guaco	*Herpetotherea cachinnans*	laughing falcon
lora	*Lepidochelys olivacea*	pacific ridley sea turtle
mapache	*Procyon lotor*	raccoon
martilla	*Potus flavus*	kinkajou
mono carablanca	*Cebus capucinus*	white-faced monkey
mono colorado	*Ateles geoffroyi*	spider monkey
mono congo	*Alouatta palliatta*	howler monkey
murcielago lengualarga	*Glossophaga soricina*	nectar bat
pelicano pardo	*Pelecanus occidentalis*	brown pelican
pizote	*Nasua narica*	coati
puma	*Eira barbara*	mountain lion
saino	*Tayassu tajacu*	collared peccary
sapo grande	*Bufo marinus*	marine toad
tepazcuintle	*Agouti paca*	paca
timburil	*Sphoeroides spp.*	puffer fish
toledo	*Chiroxiphia linearis*	long-tailed manakin
tortuga verde	*Chelonia mydas*	green sea turtle
vampiro	*Desmodus rotundus*	vampire bat
venado cola blanco	*Odocoileus virginianus*	white-tailed deer

Table 5
A small sampling of Curú's animal species. Counts are (at least) 222 bird species, 42 fish species, 24 mollusk species, 18 crustacean species, 60 mammal species, and an uncounted number of arachnid and insect species.

Table 6 (below)
Curú has over 250 tree species. Some are native to Costa Rica, others have been planted and may or may not be native. El Bosque Seco—tropical dry forests—are semi-deciduous, short forests with canopies reaching 20–30 m. Understories can reach 10–20 m, and its trees are generally slow growing with hard woods. Woody vines and bromeliad epiphytes often grow on trees.

Caoba *Swietenia humilis* mahogany	high quality woodworking; scarce
Cenicero *Philtecolobium saman* rain tree	used for banisters, interior tables; pasture shade tree, seeds dispersed by cattle; white-faced monkeys use sap as insect repellent
Cortes amarillo *Godmania*	hard wood with gold flowers, which howler monkeys like; source of food for white-faced monkeys
Guacimo *Gauzuma ulmifolia*	fast growing; only females produce fruit; endangered in Costa Rica; seeds dispersed by animal excrement
Guancaste *Enterolobium cyclocarpum*	good for furniture; shade for cattle; Costa Rica's national tree
Guapinol *Hymenacea coubaril*	resin forms amber; one of Costa Rica's largest tree species
Jobo *Spondia mombin*	soft wood; edible fruit
Palma coyol *Acrocomia vinifera*	fruit used to make wine; wood is fire resistent
Pochote *Bombacopsis quinata*	excellent for building, living fenceposts; "Curú" is local name

Almendro *Andira inermis* almond	used in building construction; fruits feed animals
Ceiba *Ceiba pentandra* kapok	soft wood, fast growing; seed fibers used in life preservers, pillows, insulation, and as protein for cattle
Espavel *Anacardium excelsum*	soft wood used for boxes, dugout canoes; pigs eat fruit
Higueron (Matapalo) *Ficus* sp. fig tree	wildlife like fruit; large buttress roots
Palma real *Scheelia rostrata* royal palm	leaves used for thatch roofing; oil in fruit
Piper *Piper* sp.	herbaceous; fruits dispersed by bats; relatively unstudied
Platanillo *Heliconia latispatha* wild plantain	leaves used for thatch; pollinated by hummingbirds; birds like fruit

Table 7 (above)
El Bosque Humédo—tropical moist forest—is Costa Rica's most common forest type. Canopies reach 40–50 m, with trunks up to 100 cm. Sub-canopies are 30 m, with understories between 8–20 m. Abundant vines and epiphytes, but few herbs due to lack of light.

Bracharia *Bracharia decumbens*	Pasture grass, good forage; resistant in dry areas
Coco *Cocos nucifera* coconut	Endoder makes coconut oil; only squirrels and kinkajous can eat the unopened fruit; used to feed pigs
Yerba Estrella *Cynodon plechostachyun* African star grass	Good forage and pasture grass; resistant in dry areas
Palma Aceitera *Elaeis guinensis* African oil palm	Used to make cooking oil (palm oil); palm nuts fed to pigs
Jaragua *Hyparrhenia rufa* jaragua	Pasture rather than forage grass; from Africa; aggressive, easily invades pastures; good for dry areas
Mango *Mangifera indica* mango	Cultivated extensively; edible fruit; pesticide necessary for cultivation; white-faced monkeys eat insect pests
Papaya *Carica papaya* papaya	Cultivated extensively; fruit edible for humans and wildlife
Platano plantain	Cultivated extensively; fruit edible for humans and wildlife
Teca *Tectona grandis* teak	Valuable, fast-growing tree species from Burma; requires a dry season; howler monkeys particularly like this tree; fallen leaves kill undergrowth

Table 8 (below)
El Manglar—mangrove forest—is both the forest name and the name of the wood found there. Mangrove forests are found at the mouths of rivers on sea coasts where salt meets fresh water. Mangroves can: protect water quality by acting as a filter; serve as wildlife nurseries; and protect against erosion.

Table 9 (right)
Trees and plants planted by people are found in pastures and fruit and tree plantations. Living fences are planted with native species, such as pochote, listed in Table 6.

Mangle botoncito buttonwood mangrove	shrubby mangrove species
Mangle pinuelo *Pelliciera rhizophorae* tea mangrove	distinguished from other mangroves by slightly buttressed trunk
Mangle rojo *Rhizophra harrizonii*	bark used for tannin; firewood; prop roots aid in respiration, and provide shelter from predation for animals
Mangle salado *Avicennia germinans* black mangrove	pneumataphores, specialized roots growing upward out of mud, that aid respiration

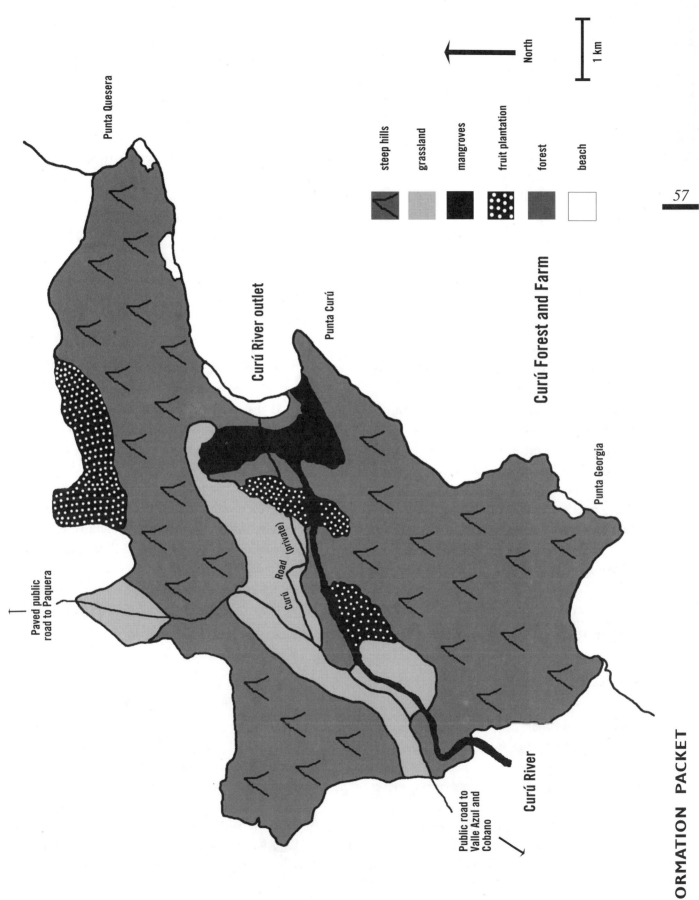

Curú Forest and Farm

Punta Quesera

Curú River outlet

Punta Curú

Punta Georgia

Paved public road to Paquera

Curú Road (private)

Curú River

Public road to Valle Azul and Cobano

	steep hills
	grassland
	mangroves
	fruit plantation
	forest
	beach

North

1 km

Biodiversity

INFORMATION PACKET

A1: Cattle Rancher

You own two large cattle ranches in Guanacaste. You bought most of your property in the 1960s when government subsidies for land clearing and ranching were high. Seventy percent of your beef is sold on the Costa Rican market. You want more land to increase profits. Curú might be a good location for expanding your business.

In your favor: Banks should loan you money. Lenders have always favored cattle ranchers and large land owners. There may still be some government subsidies available. Because you own over 1,000 hectares you can afford to practice rotational grazing which reduces erosion. Ranching doesn't require many workers, so costs are low.

Concerns: Over the last few years, the number of ranching subsidies has declined. Will anyone, including the government, object if you cut forest to expand pastures? Curú's cattle herd is very high quality. Would they sell it to you with the land?

A2: Agricultural Researcher

You are a researcher for *CATIE* (KAH-tee-ay), *Centro Agronómico Tropical de Investigación y Enseñanza* or Center for Tropical Agriculture and Teaching in Turrialba. You are an expert in pasture management and work with ranchers to improve yields. Recently you discovered a new mixture of pasture grass which will double the kilograms/hectare of beef produced annually. Most of these grasses do best in wet climates.

In your favor: You are trained in genetic research and how to apply genetic information to creating new products. If ranchers use the grasses you have developed, they can improve the amount of beef produced per hectare, meaning less land will need to be used for ranching. Cattle ranching can be considered better than growing crops, like corn, beans, or rice, in rows. Ranching requires less machinery and fewer pesticides, which is better for the soil and water supply.

Concerns: If cattle are overgrazed on steep slopes erosion can become a problem, especially in places with torrential rains. Pasture grasses may not protect soils as well as forests, and many environmentalists think cattle ranching leads to rain forest destruction. How can you convince them your new discovery can actually help reverse that? How can you convince cattle ranchers to try your ideas?

A3: Day Laborer

You are a day laborer at Curú. You come every day and do odd jobs on the farm including fence repair, planting, harvesting, and cutting grass. This job supports your family in Valle Azul.

In your favor: You are familiar with the local environment and ecology. You have a good record as a laborer at Curú. The new owners might rehire you.

Concerns: If Curú is sold and more land is converted either to forest or pasture there may be fewer jobs available on the property. Will you lose your job? You need a steady income to support your family. Will a job with the new owner provide employment all year or only seasonally?

B1: Campesino Leader

You are the leader of a women's organization in a community of landless *campesinos* (farmers). There are about 100 families in the community, all of whom migrated from the Caribbean Coast after losing their jobs and homes when banana plantations bought their land and didn't provide jobs for everyone. The women's organization represents the women's concerns in the community, including family health care, access to education, small businesses, resource collection, and food cooperatives. The organization makes sure women's concerns are considered.

In your favor: Your are a large, organized group and you can accomplish more than you could individually by pooling your money, working together, protesting, etc. The Costa Rican government has established policies to help poor farmers buy land. Each family has a few farm animals and income from day-labor jobs. Everyone has agricultural experience, and everyone is knowledgable about the local ecosystem. Perhaps you could find a way to help your organization by using that knowledge?

Concerns: Because you work 16 hour days, you want to live somewhere where most resources—including wood, fruit, agricultural land, game, and fresh water—are nearby. Banks will not lend money to your families to buy land. How will you get collateral to qualify for a loan? Where else might you get money?

B2: Day Laborer

You are the wage earner of a family of six. You are part of a community of 100 landless families from the Caribbean Coast. The families meet once a month to discuss issues that concern you, including wages, housing, finances, and available farmland. You work as a day laborer at Curú right now. Your dream is to buy a small plot of arable land for your family—about 5 hectares would be enough. It is hard to find land these days, though. Three-fourths of the land in Costa Rica is owned by only 13 percent of the population.

In your favor: Before you lost your land on the Caribbean Coast you did subsistence farming. You grew enough corn, rice, beans, plantains, cassava, and oranges for your family. You also grew some high-value crops to sell. You are an experienced farmer, you know where the good land is at Curú, and you know what crops can be grown there. You know a lot about the local ecosystem, and you are willing to learn more.

Concerns: Your family is large. If you buy land, you will have to divide it amongst your children when they marry. If you could afford it, you'd buy a larger plot. How will you purchase land? You can't afford to buy all of Curú. Banks won't loan you money because you have no collateral.

B3: JUNAFORCA Organizer

You are an organizer of *JUNAFORCA* (hoo-nah-FORK-ah), *Junta Nacional Forestal Campesina* or National Forest Campesino Group, a Costa Rican organization that helps *campesino* (farmer) groups with agriculture and forestry. *JUNAFORCA* provides information on ways to get money for land purchases and helps train people in forestry and agriculture.

In your favor: You have connections with European non-governmental organizations that provide funding to organized *campesino* groups with management plans. You know that Costa Rica's *IDA* (*Instituto de Desarrollo Agrario*) has a number of programs to help *campesinos* purchase land and finance agricultural and forestry programs. You have connections with INBio, which is always looking for people to train and educate so they can help them with their efforts.

Concerns: What type of training will the people you work with need in order to use the land wisely? Does the group have a good management plan to help them qualify for grants? How can a group of *campesinos* afford such a large piece of property?

C1: Resort Developer

You are a partner in Marceló, a European company that builds hotel-resorts all over the world. Your newest resort opened two years ago on a 2,350 hectare property on Costa Rica's Nicoya Peninsula. The resort has 400 guest rooms, a dining hall, bar, riding stable, and ecological park. Marceló is proud to be responsible for the economic development of the local community. This hotel provided much needed employment for local people. Tourists bring money to the community. Marceló plans to build more resorts in Costa Rica in the future, perhaps in Curú.

In your favor: Banks will loan you money because you have always been reliable and your credit is good. You have investors in your multimillion-dollar developments, especially Europeans and Americans. Through your Tambor resort you made friends with local and federal politicians, they like your business and will probably support you in the future. With your other resort you began a transportation and supply system.

Concerns: Some people may claim your developments are illegal and harmful to the mangrove and marine environments. Legal fights could be expensive. Does Marceló want another resort close to its old one? Is there enough labor? Would you make enough money? The current owners have a rustic tourist setting. What are tourists looking for? You build luxury accommodations, not rustic lodges.

C2: Paquera Business Association President

You are president of the Paquera (pah-CARE-ah) Business Association, and you represent all the businesses in Paquera, a town five kilometers north of Curú.

In your favor: Tourism has improved the town's economic situation. There are more businesses than before and the road is now paved all the way to Valle Azul (BYE-ay ah-SOOL). Tourism to Montezuma, Tambor, and Curú brings people through Paquera, where Curú's current owners buy supplies. The new owners may do the same.

Concerns: Would a large tourism development at Curú take business away from Paquera's stores, restaurants, and hotels? What do typical tourists want? Do they want plush accommodations or a wilderness experience? Is the area's biological diversity an attraction to be conserved?

C3: Valle Azul Mother

You are the mother of four children in the town of Valle Azul (BYE-ay ah-SOOL). Your family settled here in the early 1970s with the *precaristas*. You have a small house with a small field in which to grow some corn, rice, beans, and plantain for your own food. You sell fruit from your mango and papaya trees for extra income. Your husband works as a day laborer at Curú. Sometimes at night he illegally hunts deer and other animals on the property for food (the current owners don't allow anyone to hunt or gather resources on the property). Several of your children are trained as tour guides, and your oldest is currently away at Guanacaste National Park where he is learning how to be a paratoxonomist. Your family's survival is tied to Curú and its resources.

In your favor: Curú is nearby. You are familiar with its plants, animals, and the local ecology. Your children are also.

Concerns: Will the new owners hire your children and husband? If they do, will they pay more? Their current wages are low. Although you own a house and small parcel of property, you have to work very hard to get by.

D1: Forest Conservancy Vice President

You are Vice President of the Forest Conservancy, a non-profit organization interested in land preservation, especially forests. You are based in the United States but you have purchased property throughout North, Central, and South America. The Forest Conservancy is especially interested in preserving the few remaining patches of tropical forest in order to protect habitats containing biological diversity.

In your favor: Your membership is always growing, reaching 500,000 this year. Dues and contributions are sufficient to purchase large properties. Because Curú is biologically diverse, your board of directors is likely to approve its

purchase. The owners know your organization because of their interest in forest protection.

Concerns: Agriculture currently divides the forest in two. For certain species, such as the mountain lion, there should be one large forest. How much does reforestation cost? Would the government pay for it? You acquire nearly 100 properties a year and often rely on land contributions or reduced prices to purchase and manage so many projects. The current owners hire guards to protect the property from illegal hunting and tree cutting. Should you hire guards? Can you afford them? How will you manage the land if you buy it? You don't live in Costa Rica.

D2: ASCONA Member

You are a member of *ASCONA* (ah-SCONE-ah), *Asociacion para la Conservación de la Naturaleza* or Association for the Conservation of Nature, an environmental activist group on Costa Rica's Nicoya Peninsula. You tried to stop construction of nearby Tambor Resort, but failed. This large deve-lopment threatens sea turtle nests, mangrove habitat, and water quality, among other things. Your group is an "environmental watch dog" on the Peninsula.

In your favor: You are organized. You know Costa Rica's forest and coastal protection laws and can use them to fight improper developments.

The government can declare certain areas as protected lands so they can't be developed. You are local and have the support of local people.

Concerns: Will the new owners of Curú build another resort? How can you get money to fight them? Your group doesn't have a lot of money to fight big companies. Many people in local communities like Tambor Resort because they got jobs and the community now has more money. How do you deal with local people who like development because of this? They don't see how new developments can harm the environment.

D3: Paquera School Teacher

You teach elementary school in Paquera. The Costa Rican Ministry of Education requires all schools to teach environmental education. Part of this requirement is a visit to a natural area. For the past five years, you have led annual field trips to Curú to teach about wildlife and conservation.

In your favor: It takes only 15 minutes to get to Curú. The current owners spend a lot of time

and money helping your environmental education program. They helped teach the children about conservation.

Concerns: What will the new owners do to Curú? Will they cut down the forest? Will they let the children visit? Your students would be outraged if anything happened to Curú. They appreciate its wildlife and beauty.

E1: Investment Manager

You represent a small group of investors from San José interested in buying land. The investors are lawyers, doctors, and other professionals. They want you to buy a piece of property and hire a manager. They hope the land will increase in value so they can sell at a large profit in the future.

In your favor: Your investors have enough money to buy large pieces of property. They are eligible for bank loans. Costa Rica gives tax breaks to those who reforest. If the land you buy could avoid property taxes, your profits would be higher.

You need to investigate other government incentives. This is a unique property, and its value is likely to rise.

Concerns: The current owners are using the property for agriculture, ranching, tourism, and forestry. Which of these activities is the best money maker? What do local people want? You want to avoid potentially expensive conflicts. You are not, however, concerned with providing many jobs.

- -

E2: Logging Company Owner

You own a small, local logging company. You harvest high-value timber for different clients. Land is often used for cattle ranching after you cut, a profitable business from what you hear. Your own business has been successful and you have earned enough money to buy a few hectares and build a home. You'd like to harvest timber at Curú, but its owners have sold only a little.

In your favor: Tropical timber is valuable on the international market. You are an experienced logger and know the most profitable techniques for timber extraction.

Concerns: Which high-value timber species does Curú contain? What are the laws on extraction? Would you be willing to cut timber illegally? Over 50 percent of timber cut on private lands in Costa Rica is cut without a permit. The government doesn't usually catch those who do that.

- -

E3: Forest Manager

You are a forest manager. You like to think about the forest's future and how to keep it valuable 50 or 100 years from now, even if trees are cut for timber. You know what types of management techniques are best to help grow high-value tree species and those important to wildlife. Some tree species that are good for wildlife can't be sold for profit right now. You prefer using species native to Costa Rica because they do best in the natural forest ecosystem.

In your favor: Many new policies in Costa Rica provide money for forest regeneration and management. If valuable species aren't on the land right now, they can be planted for future harvesting.

Concerns: There are a number of unique forest systems at Curú. Coastal areas, mangrove forests, and steepy sloped areas need to be carefully treated. Tree harvests and roads used to remove trees should be well planned to prevent erosion. Will the new owners stop managing the forest and just cut everything? If they do, the forest won't grow back well. How can you convince people that your ideas and forest management techniques, which are grounded in a scientific understanding of Curú's ecology, can keep the forest ecosystems healthy even though you are seen to be cutting trees?

F: Legal Expert

You are a legal expert. Your first job is to learn Costa Rica's laws and decrees—you will be given a copy. You will then work as a consultant evaluating land proposals and deciding whether or not they are legal. You are impartial and you don't play favorites. You must explain the laws to people with less expertise. You can make recommendations to help people improve their proposals. Here are your duties:

1. Read through the Costa Rican Laws and Decrees. They come in three sections: Forests, Agriculture, and Conservation.
2. Work with the other Legal Experts to understand exactly what each law means. For some laws it will help if you draw a picture to explain them (for example Forestry Law D and Conservation Law C).
3. Determine criteria a land proposal must pass in order to be considered legal. Use the Legal Points to Consider checklist to guide you as you review a land-use proposal.
4. You will consult with one group of prospective buyers. They will show you their proposal. Determine if it is legal. If the group has neglected a law, explain to them what needs to be done. If you have any other suggestions, feel free to give them. You are impartial and should only give LEGAL suggestions.
5. Once you determine that a proposal is legal, fill out the top portion of a Certificate of Legal and Financial Viability and sign it. This gives the prospective buyers permission to present their proposal—they keep the certificate.

- -

G: Owners

Stop playing the role of legal expert and take on the role of a member of the Schutt-Valle family, Curú's owners. You are responsible as a family for deciding who gets to buy Curú. Before you hear the final proposals talk about your priorities for selling. Do you care how the new owners use Curú? What is an acceptable price? Do you want to sell it in one piece? You may choose to play one of the following family members:

Don Federico Schutt—father and Curú's original purchaser. You lived on this land for over 60 years and you will find it very hard to sell. You spent much of your life regenerating the forest in valuable timber trees. You've always had very good business sense, and you knew how to keep the agricultural and forest enterprises going.

Doña Julieta Schutt-Valle—mother. You handle the finances of the business. All the money always goes through you. Like your husband you know every square centimeter of Curú. You can name all its animals and you know many medicinal uses for its plants. You are strong and you enjoy working outdoors.

Adelina Schutt-Valle—oldest child, age 28. You do a little bit of everything on the property. You started the environmental education program in the schools and have helped patch up relations with the neighboring towns. You supervise Curú's conservation and restoration work. When biologists come to study at Curú, you work with them. Protecting wildlife is very important to you.

Federico Schutt-Valle—middle child, age 27. You helped your father with forest regeneration, harvesting, and protection. You often worked with the guards when they patrol. You have always enjoyed the solitude of Curú's beach. Now you spend most of your time in San José and visit only on weekends.

Luis Schutt-Valle—youngest child, age 25. You've always helped with Curú's cattle ranching and agriculture. You enjoy riding horses and caring for animals. Cattle have always been important at Curú. They bring in a large part of the family income. Like your brother, you now spend most of your time in San José.

Certificate of
Legal and Financial Viability

I hereby certify that the land-use proposal developed by

_____

is legal and abides by the Costa Rica Laws and Decrees.

Signed: _____, *Legal Expert,*

on the _____ *day of the month of* _____ *in the year*_____.

I hereby certify that the land-use proposal developed by

_____

*shall be financed in such manner as to afford success
within the limits of the current economic system.*

Signed: _____, *Financial Expert,*

on the _____ *day of the month of* _____ *in the year*_____.